CAREERS FOR

BOOK WORMS

& Other Literary Types

VGM Careers for You Series

CAREERS FOR
BOOK
WORMS
& Other Literary Types

MARJORIE EBERTS
MARGARET GISLER

THIRD EDITION

VGM Career Books

Chicago   New York   San Francisco   Lisbon   London   Madrid   Mexico City
Milan   New Delhi   San Juan   Seoul   Singapore   Sydney   Toronto

Library of Congress Cataloging-in-Publication Data

Eberts, Marjorie.
    Careers for bookworms & other literary types / Marjorie Eberts and Margaret
Gisler.— 3rd ed.
        p.   cm. — (VGM careers for you series)
    Includes bibliographical references.
    ISBN 0-07-139031-6 (pbk.)
      1. Book industries and trade—Vocational guidance—United States.
2. Publishers and publishing—Vocational guidance—United States.
3. Information science—Vocational guidance—United States.   4. Library science—
Vocational guidance—United States.   5. Research—Vocational guidance—United
States.   I. Title: Careers for bookworms and other literary types.   II. Gisler,
Margaret.   III. Title.   IV. Series.

Z471.E25   2002
381'.45002'023—dc21   2002024996

1 2 3 4 5 6 7 8 9 0   LBM/LBM   1 0 9 8 7 6 5 4 3 2

ISBN 0-07-139031-6

This book is printed on acid-free paper.

*To Patty White, our favorite bookworm,
who reads books, hoards books, and
keeps them as friends forever*

Contents

Acknowledgments

···

We wish to thank Kevin Crider for providing substantial help in the revision of this book. We also appreciate the help of the many bookworms who shared personal stories of careers that truly let them read on the job.

CHAPTER ONE

Career Possibilities for Bookworms

Finding Reading Jobs

Welcome to the Information Age—the perfect time for bookworms and other literary types to be looking for careers that involve reading. Never before have there been so many printed materials to read. Plus, there is the new kid on the block—the Internet—with millions of pages to be explored. No matter where you live, whether it is in a huge city or a small rural community, chances are high that you will be able to combine avocation with vocation in some way and find a career that really lets you read on the job.

As a bookworm, you will be delighted to know that your love of the printed page is rapidly spreading to more and more people. With the publication of exciting new books, young children throughout the world have suddenly discovered how magical it is to read. Their enthusiasm even extends at times to eschewing television for reading. Many will probably join you as members of that special breed of people known as bookworms.

It is not difficult to recognize bookworms. They are the ones with their noses buried in books on buses and planes. They read while eating a solitary lunch in a cafeteria. They read at swimming pools, on park benches, and even in front of television sets. Libraries and bookstores are their second homes. Wherever there are books, there will be bookworms close by.

A bookworm's passion for the printed word never cools—even though he or she has read hundreds of books and handled thousands more. They are entranced by great literature, captivated by mysteries, enthralled by biographies, fascinated by histories, attracted to nonfiction, and drawn to all books, from encyclopedias to bestsellers. They are the most educated people on Earth.

The longer bookworms live with books, the more the magnetism of books draws them into reading more and more titles. They enjoy relaxing with books, shopping for books, collecting books, and sharing them with friends. They share the cherished dream to find jobs that let them be paid to read.

A Bookworm's Dream—Reading from Nine to Five

When bookworms read help wanted ads in newspapers and magazines and on websites, they are always looking for that special job that will allow them to spend even more time reading. If they search the ads carefully, they will find appealing jobs like these:

- **Radio Show Producer:** Popular talk-show host seeks fast reader with solid knowledge of pop culture to select show topics. Job includes screening calls from listeners.
- **Book Reviewer:** Newspaper needs reader to write book reviews for Sunday edition. Must have strong writing skills.
- **Research Assistant:** University wants specialist on Middle East history to work as member of team creating position papers for government agency.
- **Acquisitions Librarian:** Major public library seeks qualified librarian to select books to add to children's collection at main and branch libraries. Must be familiar with trends in children's literature.
- **Legislative Analyst:** Senate seeks analyst to work on welfare subcommittee to evaluate new programs. Strong research skills required.

- **Information Broker:** Large law firm needs individual with some legal experience to do online searching for trademark and patent information.

A Glimpse at Possible Jobs

Several years ago, a confirmed bookworm was browsing through the first edition of this book hoping to find a job that involved substantial amounts of reading. When she chanced to read the section on special libraries, she immediately knew that this was the place where she wanted to work. Today, this bookworm is happily reading on the job as research manager of the library at *BusinessWeek* magazine. In Chapter 2, you will read about how she got this job and how much reading she is fortunate to do at work every day. We hope this book will help you discover a job that will let you be paid for reading. Here is a bird's-eye view of some of the jobs you will read about in this book.

Careers in Libraries

A job at a library is primarily a job with books—a major reason bookworms get so excited about working in libraries. Plus, no one who works in a library can adequately serve library patrons without doing some reading on the job. Because there are so many different kinds of libraries, future library employees can envision careers working in libraries at government agencies, magazines, newspapers, law offices, research centers, banks, and advertising agencies, as well as public and school libraries.

Careers in Book Publishing

The most appealing aspect of a career in book publishing is the opportunity to be part of creating a book and getting it into the hands of readers. Each step in this creation process brings jobs for bookworms interested in acquiring, editing, copyediting, proofreading, marketing, and selling books. With the number of new books being published increasing each year, opportunities abound for bookworms to find jobs at both large and small publishing companies. The easiest way to get your foot in the door at these companies is by working as an intern or taking any kind of entry-level position.

Careers with Magazines and Newspapers

Bookworms do not just bury their noses in books. They read anything that is printed, especially magazines and newspapers. Although many of the editorial jobs in magazines and newspapers are similar to those in book publishing, there are several additional jobs. Think about all the letters that magazines and newspapers receive; someone has to read them and handle them appropriately. Then research must be done to ensure that everything that is printed is accurate and that reporters have all the background information needed for their articles. Within this variety, several jobs offer bookworms the special opportunity to do nothing but read.

Careers in Glamour Industries

Bookworms are not just fascinated by the printed word. Many are drawn to jobs in the movie industry, television, radio, and public relations that offer a touch of glamour. After all, someone has to be hired to screen scripts to discover the right properties for a movie studio and to handle a superstar's mail. And behind every talk-show host on radio and television, there is usually a producer reading like crazy to find topics that will grab an audience. There are even jobs for bookworms in the limelight. Some well-known television and radio personalities read continually to prepare for their broadcasts.

Careers in Education

You can't be an effective teacher without doing considerable reading to increase your knowledge. Classroom teachers have to read textbooks and accompanying teachers' manuals, professional journals, books, and magazines to enrich the curriculum for their students. University professors have to read and research to obtain their doctorates. Then they must continue reading and researching to publish scholarly works that will help them achieve tenure. In fact, the higher the teaching level, the more reading you will do as part of your job.

Careers in Research

Many bookworms find research jobs to be especially satisfying as they require so much reading. Imagine yourself as a historian reading through the papers of past presidents searching for the rationale behind important political decisions. Or you could be doing research at a pharmaceutical company to find information on effective herbal cures used in the eighteenth century. While jobs in research were once found primarily at universities, there are now abundant opportunities for research with the government, businesses, and think tanks. Many of these jobs involve an extensive amount of work with computer databases.

Careers with the Government

Because the government is the largest single employer in the United States with a workforce of twenty million civilian workers, bookworms are likely to find many jobs that appeal to them in the public sector. The career options are endless, as the government employs people in just about every occupation the private sector does, as well as many found only in the public sector. At the federal and state levels, you could work for a senator or representative reading mail and handling constituent requests. On the local level, you could spend your time helping people search for property titles and more. Overall, your best chance for employment with the government is at the local level because this is where most of the jobs are.

Careers in the Private Sector

With the explosion of information, almost every profession from engineering to medicine requires more reading by professionals. All large companies are looking for people to manage information and to retrieve needed information. One of the fastest-growing businesses today is information services. Because the private sector is where the greatest number of jobs are, this is where bookworms will find the most jobs that let them be paid to read. From Wall Street to telecommuting on a hilltop, there are appealing jobs in the private sector for readers like you.

More Career Opportunities for Bookworms

Bookworms tend to look for jobs that involve reading at places where books are traditionally found: libraries, schools, and publishing companies. While it is true that many jobs for readers are found in these places, many other opportunities exist that let you do a lot of reading on the job. However, it does take some investigation to discover these jobs. Bookworms may be perfect for jobs as translators, storytellers, genealogy researchers, and news clippers for individuals and companies. Then, of course, there is the ideal job for a true bookworm—being an author and writing books.

....

Job Qualifications

Bookworms speak frequently and eloquently about their love for books. They consider books not only as prized possessions but also as true friends. However, a love of books and reading is not sufficient qualification for many jobs that require a significant amount of reading. Education really counts. In many cases, having a bachelor's degree isn't even enough. Quite often a master's degree is a prerequisite for being considered for a position. And there are many jobs for bookworms where holding double master's degrees or a doctorate would be helpful. Fortunately, bookworms tend to want to study and receive as much education as possible. In preparing for a career, bookworms also need to realize that most reading jobs now require sophisticated computer skills.

....

For Further Reading

John Adams demonstrated how well he knew what it was like to be a bookworm when he stated, "I read my eyes out and can't read half enough. . . . The more one reads the more one sees we have to read." Bookworms should become familiar with career books like these in searching for the perfect job.

Ackley, Kristina M. *100 Top Internet Job Sites: Get Wired, Get Hired in Today's New Job Market.* Big Bear City, CA: Impact Publishing, 2000.

Allen, Jeffrey G. *The Complete Q&A Job Interview Book.* New York: John Wiley & Sons, 2000.

The Big Book of Jobs. Chicago: VGM Career Books, 2003.

Bloch, Jay A., and Michael Betrus. *101 More Best Resumes.* Chicago: VGM Career Books, 1999.

Bolles, Richard Nelson. *Job Hunting on the Internet.* Berkeley, CA: Ten Speed Press, 2001.

Dikel, M. *Guide to Internet Job Searching.* Chicago: VGM Career Books, 2002.

Kaplan, Robbie Miller. *How to Say It in Your Job Search.* Paramus, NJ: Prentice Hall, 2002.

Krannich, Ronald L. *Change Your Job, Change Your Life.* Waupaca, WI: Impact Publications, 2000.

Krannich, Ronald L., and Caryl Rae Krannich. *Savvy Networker: Building Your Job Net for Success.* Waupaca, WI: Impact Publications, 2001.

United States Department of Labor. *Occupational Outlook Handbook.* Chicago: VGM Career Books, 2002.

Washington, Tom. *Interview Power.* Bellevue, WA: Mt. Vernon Press, 2000.

CHAPTER TWO

Careers in Libraries

Working Closely with Books

C an there possibly be a more perfect workplace for bookworms than a library? No other career will let you hang out with stacks of books as well as fellow bookworms eager to read and garner all types of information. Wherever you work, be it the immense Library of Congress with more than twenty-four million books or a school library with several thousand volumes, you will always be surrounded by books. Plus, there is one other great reward with a career in a library: you will be helping others access vital personal knowledge, whether it is the next Drew Carey looking for books on how to write jokes or a diabetes patient searching for a treatment database.

Today, there are more than 122,000 libraries of all kinds in the United States. The work opportunities are almost endless. Besides employing librarians and other professionals, libraries also have a variety of jobs for support staff.

If you decide to work in a library, you will be in good company. Aristotle is probably the first well-known librarian. He gathered a collection of books for his school in Athens, founded in 347 B.C. Before that, libraries of papyrus scrolls and clay tablets were cared for by librarians as long ago as 2000 B.C. In the British Museum, you can actually see an ancient library of clay tablets that was organized by an Assyrian king in about 700 B.C. And for a short time in recent years, an American astronaut even set up a small library on the Mir space station.

Two famous colonial figures, Benjamin Franklin and Thomas Jefferson, were also librarians. Pinch-penny Franklin started a subscription library, limiting circulation to subscribers who paid a yearly fee. Not only did Jefferson catalog and classify materials for the University of Virginia library, his own personal library had ten thousand books. After the first Library of Congress burned, Jefferson's collection became the nucleus of the new library.

Familiar modern figures who were librarians include J. Edgar Hoover, who worked at the Library of Congress while completing his law degree, and Mao Tse-tung, who was a library assistant at the Beijing University library. Mao carried periodicals to readers' tables and earned the same salary as a coolie.

Books are a librarian's major business. From four thousand years ago until today, the focus of the librarian's job is much the same. Librarians collect, organize, and make information available to people. What is new to the job is the important role technology plays in the work.

Taking a Good Look at the Workplace

When you choose to work as a librarian, it may not always be in a modern, comfortable, spacious environment. You may drive all day in a bookmobile, work next door to a laboratory with all its varied odors, or hand out books at a remote army base. There is a remarkable assortment of libraries in the United States, usually divided into these four categories: public, school, academic, and special. But no matter whether a library is located at a zoo, in a law office, in a metropolitan area, or in a small rural community, the librarian is the person who provides the essential services.

The Familiar Public Library

Bookworms are always well acquainted with the public libraries in their areas. And there is no shortage of libraries for them to visit. The United States has approximately sixteen thousand central and branch public libraries. These libraries, which are usually supported locally, vary greatly in size. You can get lost in the huge New York Public Library with its ten million books or find yourself in a small one-room library within the Arctic Circle in Alaska. However, no matter where a library is or how large or small it is, a librarian is needed to serve its users.

Regardless of size, all public libraries have the same mission of serving the people who use them. This means having at least a core of reference books for everyone in the community, plus sections for children and adults. In some areas, libraries have special sections to meet the needs of that community. For example, the Detroit Public Library has a variety of materials on the history of the automobile. And most libraries now have computers to give users access to library databases and the Internet.

Public libraries are no longer limited to traditional library buildings. In addition to roving bookmobiles, there are often services to retirement and nursing homes, jails, and hospitals.

School Libraries

The little old red schoolhouse did not have a library. However, in recent years, more and more schools have added libraries because teachers are asking their students to get information beyond what is in textbooks. Today, there are more than ninety-eight thousand school libraries.

The contents of school libraries tie closely to what is being taught at the schools. Obviously, high school libraries have a far wider range of materials than those in elementary, middle, or junior high schools. Because today's school libraries are also storehouses for films, filmstrips, recordings, videos, and graphic materials and provide access to all types of information through computers, they are now usually called library media centers or just media centers.

Academic Libraries

"Where are you going?" one college student asks another. Not surprisingly, the answer often is "the library." Students go to the library to find information, to research, and to study at the large tables or special study carrels.

Not all academic libraries are the same. Community college libraries tend to cater to the needs of adult and vocational learners. College libraries vary greatly in size and scope. The library at Harvard University, with its more than fourteen million volumes, is the second largest in the United States. However, because of library networks and interlibrary loans, students can obtain just about any book that they want. University libraries are usually the largest academic libraries. Many have very specialized collections on specific subjects. The gigantic University of California library system has collections devoted to subjects such as citrus fruits, California history, and oceanography. At a large university, you may find many separate libraries devoted to specific subjects located all over the campus.

Because of the knowledge boom that began in the 1950s and continues today, there has been a real increase in library building to store all this information. There has also been a fantastic increase in the use of computers in libraries to access all the information stored online throughout the world.

Special Libraries

Special is the key word to use in describing these libraries because they deal with specialized subjects, such as pharmacology, law, transportation, religion, and medicine. They have users who want special information, such as the federal requirements to be followed in removing asbestos or the best treatment for Parkinson's disease. Without these special libraries, people would find it impossible to keep up with the latest information in so many areas—especially in scientific fields. What follows is just a glimpse at some of the special libraries that exist, and all these libraries have jobs for librarians.

Government Libraries. The Library of Congress, the National Library of Medicine, and the Library of Agriculture are three government libraries that have developed such extensive collections that they are considered national libraries. In addition, the government operates an amazing number of libraries.

Each branch of the armed services has technical, educational, and recreational libraries on a nationwide and worldwide basis. The navy even operates libraries on board ships. You will find libraries at Veterans Administration hospitals, the National Weather Service, the Patent and Trademark Office, the Environmental Protection Agency, and in every department of the government. The states also operate their own libraries. The list of government libraries is almost endless.

Business Libraries. When employees at a firm need special information, they can often find it in the company library. Special libraries can be found in businesses such as the following:

banks
accounting firms
steel companies
public utilities
television stations
aeronautics firms
investment houses
newspapers
food-processing firms
advertising agencies
research institutes
telephone companies

Science Libraries. The vast amount of scientific knowledge that is constantly being discovered, updated, and changed in scientific fields such as nutrition, marine biology, botany, physiology, biochemistry, zoology, and the health sciences necessitates libraries in a wide range of organizations, including:

chemical companies
cosmetics companies
medical schools

health centers
hospitals
petroleum refineries
mining firms
horticultural centers
veterinary hospitals
pharmaceutical firms

Would You Really Like to Be a Librarian?

You won't become a millionaire as a librarian, but you may have the opportunity to do a lot of reading. Being a bookworm, this should please you. However, you should realize that relatively few librarians have the luxury of sitting down on the job and reading a book from cover to cover. Of course, there are exceptions, such as the bibliographer at the National Library of Congress who spent forty years reading as he worked on a bibliography of snow, ice, and permafrost.

The librarian sitting behind a desk at your local library is doing far more than reading; he or she spends a lot of time answering questions and helping patrons. But the librarian also has the chance to see new books coming into the library, read reviews of books in an assigned area in order to find books to order, and assemble book lists. And in this age of technology, the librarian is now busy searching and helping patrons find information via the computer.

Do You Have the Necessary Personal Qualifications?

Most library jobs require considerable versatility. However, there are certain qualities that most librarians share. Answer the following questions with a "yes" or a "no" to see if you possess most of these qualities.

1. Do you have a genuine love of books?
2. Do you have a wide knowledge of books?
3. Do you have the patience to keep searching until required materials are found?
4. Do you have above-average academic ability?
5. Do you have a good memory?
6. Do you possess intellectual curiosity?
7. Do you have the ability to make decisions?
8. Do you have the ability to attend carefully to details?
9. Do you like to work with computers?
10. Do you have good oral and written communication skills?
11. Do you have a willingness to accept and handle new technologies?
12. Do you possess the knack of being tactful and courteous?
13. Do you have a desire for continuing education?
14. Do you have a genuine interest in helping people use libraries?
15. Do you have the ability to get along with all types of people?

Even if you answered "yes" to all of the above questions, it does not mean that you will be happy or successful in every library position you might consider. The personal qualities that would make you an excellent corporate librarian might not make you an excellent children's librarian, for example. In addition to the necessary personal qualifications, prospective librarians need to realize that there are considerable educational requirements for the position of professional librarian.

The Education of a Librarian

The amount of education needed depends upon the job that you want to hold. If you want to be a professional librarian, you are going to have to obtain a master's degree in library and information science (M.L.S.) in order to work at most libraries. This often takes at least a year beyond the bachelor's degree, but two-year programs are becoming common. A typical graduate program includes courses in the foundations of library and information science, material selection and processing, the organization of information, reference tools and strategies, and user services. Future librarians are taught to use new resources brought about by advancing technology, such as online reference systems, Internet search methods, and automated circulation systems.

Although a number of colleges offer the M.L.S. degree, you will probably want to attend one that has a program accredited by the American Library Association. Admission to these programs isn't easy. Not only will you need good college grades (B average), you may also need an acceptable score on the Graduate Record Examination. Librarians are quite an educated group. After obtaining an M.L.S., many take courses in continuing education throughout their careers. And librarians with specific goals often go on to earn certificates for advanced study programs, master's degrees in different fields, or even doctorates in library science.

Schooling Required for Professional Librarians

Public Libraries. If you want a really high administrative post in a very large library, having a master's degree in library science may not be enough. You may find it helpful to have a Ph.D. in library science or an advanced business degree.

School Libraries. If you like working with school-age children and are seriously considering being a school librarian, check the department of education's certification requirements in the state where you want to work. It may be sufficient to have a bachelor's degree in education plus courses in library science. In some cases, you would need a master's degree in library science, perhaps with a library media specialization, or a master's in education with a specialty in school library media or education media.

Academic Libraries. Librarians wishing to teach or hold top administrative posts will find it helpful to have doctorate degrees.

Special Libraries. Not only is a special librarian going to need an M.L.S., at least a bachelor's degree or possibly another master's degree is often required in the library's special subject area.

Schooling Required for Library Support Staff

Depending on where they work, the support staff of libraries have such titles as library technicians, library technical assistants, and library paraprofessionals. These library employees certainly don't need the years of education beyond high school that professional librarians do. In fact, it is even possible to get a support staff position with just a high school diploma and on-the-job training. Many libraries, nevertheless, prefer support staff to have completed a two-year college program in library technology. Some even require a bachelor's degree.

Librarians Talk About Their Work

Librarians love to read and feel that they need to read all the time because so much new material is constantly being published. However, most librarians can't read as much as they want because they have so many other things to do on their jobs. Librarians do manage to keep current with literature in their specific areas by relying on professional journals, book lists, and reviews.

The basic tasks of librarians are largely the same whether they are working in a public, school, academic, or special library. To give you a better picture of what librarians do, some librarians describe their work on the following pages.

Acquisitions Librarian at a Central Library

Kathy Barnard may have close to the perfect job for a bookworm. As a member of the department that selects books and other materials for a large public library, she chooses the books that the library will acquire for its branches. In one year, Kathy may recommend the purchase of a few thousand new books. This does not actually involve reading books on the job but rather reading reviews of books. Her job is challenging because she has to predict how popular a book will be with library patrons before it is even released. The easiest choices are new books by well-known authors. Kathy finds this job to be very satisfying because she has the opportunity to be so immersed in the world of books. Before acquiring this job, she worked as a reference librarian.

Reference Librarian in a Suburban Library

Because she is a confirmed bookworm, Stefanie van Ogtrop loved the idea of working in a library after graduating from college. Her first job in the world of books was as a clerk—an opening she saw in the local newspaper. After obtaining her M.L.S. degree, she became a young adult librarian and established programs appealing to this age group.

Today, Stefanie is branch manager of a suburban library. When she is not handling administrative responsibilities, she takes turns with two other librarians at the reference desk. She considers the job of reference librarian similar to being a detective. With six hundred to seven hundred patrons visiting the library every day, the questions vary enormously, from a school child seeking information on a Texas governor of the 1800s to an adult looking for facts on global warming. Stefanie uses computer resources to answer many questions; however, she often finds it faster and easier to consult library books and other materials.

One of the best perks of Stefanie's job is having the chance to look at all the new books that arrive at the library. She always picks a few to browse. Her own need to read also widens her background and makes it so much easier to answer patrons' questions.

Library Administrator

The higher you climb on the administrative ladder in a library, the shorter the amount of time you are likely to read on the job. Vivian Small remembers being assigned the delightful task of reading all the award-winning Newbery and Caldecott books in one of her first jobs as a children's librarian. Plus, as both a children's librarian and a reference librarian, she spent considerable time reading reviews to select books to be added to collections. Vivian even did some reading as the manager of a branch library, where she also served as a reference librarian. She was involved in the selection of new books and helping patrons find books that they would like. One of the most enjoyable aspects of this job was going to book warehouses and wandering up and down the aisles selecting books for her branch.

When Vivian became a supervising librarian of seven libraries in a large city, her contact with books and library patrons almost entirely vanished. Her job involved hiring and training library personnel, scheduling, budgeting, maintaining the facilities, and attending meetings. Nevertheless, this confirmed bookworm, who often got into trouble as a child because she was always reading, is still an avid reader who has a book in her hands whenever she can at home.

Research Librarian at a Business Magazine

Susann Rutledge is a confirmed bookworm. In fact, her earliest childhood memory centers on being in a library. As research manager at *Business Week* magazine, she now gets paid to work in a library and read—an ideal situation for her. And she works with four researchers, two paraprofessionals, and the library director, who also read on the job.

The librarians spend their days doing research for the magazine's reporters and editorial staff who need information for their stories. As research manager, she also is responsible for keeping track of all requests that come into the office and making sure they are answered. The requests are prioritized, and the E-mail system is the primary method of tracking each request. In just a month, the researchers will answer as many as five hundred requests. While many queries cover different businesses and the stock market, plenty of others relate to politics, the entertainment industry, or advances in medicine. Most research is done online using databases.

Because there is so much information available, Susann and the other researchers have to evaluate very carefully what they have read in order to write a summary to fulfill each request. Some requests take just a few minutes to handle, while others may take hours. When research is so vital to a story that Susann becomes the reporter's right hand, she receives a byline credit. She has received credit for her work on several cover stories.

What kind of a background do you need to get a job like Susann's? She and the other librarians all have master's degrees in library and information science. How do you get these jobs that let you read? Most of the staff members sent unsolicited resumes to the magazine. Susann had a summer internship in which she was able to demonstrate her solid research skills, and she was offered a full-time job after graduation. She recommends this job to anyone who loves to read and learn new things every day.

Reference Librarian in a Newspaper Library

The major purpose of a newspaper library is to provide a story archive, according to Dawn Hall, who handles several jobs in the library of a large newspaper. "It's very concise, exact, and fast reading," she says. As an indexer, Dawn is assigned several pages of the newspaper to read carefully. She selects the stories the newspaper will want to keep on file in the electronic library system. Next, the paper goes to data processing, where each story is called up in the electronic archive for enhancement with categories, topics, art captions, keywords, and other information to make retrieval as easy as possible. Then Dawn or another processor compares the electronic text to the published text to confirm that they match.

The last step is for the processor to sign off on the story and send it to the story archive.

Dawn spends from one and a half to four hours a day indexing and data processing stories. The rest of her time is spent doing research to answer questions for reporters. She also compiles reference statistics that are used to track source needs, slow and busy times and days, and user requests. Because the newspaper library is open from 7 A.M. to midnight, Dawn and the other staff members work shifts.

Dawn's background includes a bachelor's degree in education and a master's degree in library and information science. Two of her coworkers and the head librarian also have M.L.S. degrees. Dawn worked at a small newspaper after college before she found this job through a want ad in the newspaper.

Manager of Library and Information Services at a Zoo

Suzanne Braun-McKee actually found her job as a zoo librarian through a newspaper ad that piqued her interest. She had the rare opportunity of building a brand-new library and developing a collection of books, journals, videos, and slides. It has also been her responsibility to continually expand the zoo's library to meet staff needs. In doing her job, she has had to become an expert on materials ranging from orchids to rhinos.

To be successful in the special library field, Suzanne has found it essential to use diverse reading skills. She spends a lot of time on the Web sifting through information for the zoo curators. Then, she has to use her critical-thinking skills and library background to determine what information is accurate and reliable. Much of her reading is of very technical materials, requiring her to analyze carefully what she has read.

As manager of the zoo library, Suzanne has had to become a jack-of-all-trades as she juggles several duties that you might not expect a librarian to handle. She proofreads all the publications of the zoo, writes interpretive information signs, creates handouts for general visitors, and sits on a lot of committees.

While Suzanne loves to read, her major reason for becoming a librarian was to disseminate knowledge. At the zoo, she is able to turn what she reads into helping the staff and general public find out what they want to know.

Library Director at a Law Office

A virtual library is not enough for lawyers; they still need law books. The large Midwestern firm where Nikki Schofield works has more than ten thousand volumes. Two other full-time librarians work with her to handle the requests of the attorneys. The librarians also do such things as shelving books, filing new material, and keeping track of circulation. As director of the library, Nikki has the additional tasks of training staff and deciding what databases the firm will subscribe to.

Nikki's job is perfect for someone who loves to read because it is her major activity. And it also presents an opportunity for her to use her research skills as she finds information such as the following for the lawyers:

- precedent-setting dog-bite cases
- a list of all pending federal cases on intellectual property
- the biographies of opposing attorneys
- the reputation of a newspaper

Nikki describes her job as challenging and never boring. She continues to hone her skills, focusing most of her attention on classes to learn new technology. When her workday is over, this bookworm just transfers her attention to reading books on the Civil War—her favorite avocation.

School Library Media Coordinator

What makes Joanne Fox's job satisfying as an elementary school librarian is the opportunity to teach children how to use the library and to acquaint them with the world of books. Every day several classes come to the library. Joanne typically begins each half-hour session by reading and discussing an age-appropriate story with the children. Then time is spent on building their library skills before she helps them select books.

Besides working with the students, Joanne also helps the teachers select books to match their classroom curriculums. Plus, time needs to be spent every day handling administrative tasks and directing the volunteer aides.

Considerable reading is involved in this job, as Joanne has to decide which books should be added to the library's collection of ten thousand volumes. Then when the new books arrive, this bookworm always tries to read all the picture books and novels and as many other books as she can. As a result, she always has a stack of books by her bed at home.

In order to be a school librarian in her state, it was only necessary for Joanne to have a bachelor's degree. The principal chose her for this job because of her superior qualifications. She also had master's degrees in zoology and museum studies and had worked part-time in a public library.

The Good and Bad of Being a Librarian

Just like any other career, being a librarian has both positive and negative aspects. While this career may not let bookworms read as much as they like, it does allow them to spend time near their fondest possessions—books.

Good Things About Being a Librarian

1. Part of the time in your job you will be paid for doing what you love most—reading.
2. You will be working with people who share your love of books.
3. You will have the opportunity to share your knowledge of books with library patrons.

4. You will be joining a profession that demands you keep learning about what is happening in the world.
5. You will have a job that lets you use all your creativity and initiative in searching for hard-to-find materials.
6. You can choose to be either a generalist or a specialist who concentrates on a particular field of interest.
7. You can choose between working with people or working for the most part by yourself.
8. You can feel the reward of furthering other people's knowledge, whether they are esoteric researchers or third graders doing their first reports.

Things to Consider About Being a Librarian
1. Considerable preparation is required for this career; librarians usually need to have master's degrees.
2. Pay for librarians is not always equal to that of other professions that require the same amount of schooling.
3. You may have to cope at times with unreasonable demands and discourteous behavior from library patrons.
4. You may have to be able to stoop, lift, and stretch as you shelve or reach for books.
5. You will have to be willing to use computers in searching for information at most libraries.
6. You will not always work the typical nine-to-five day. Libraries are open in the evenings and on weekends.

Getting a Job as a Librarian
If you just want a clerical or a technical job in a library, you can usually find this type of work by contacting a local library or reading newspaper ads. Here are some possible career paths to follow.

Part-Time Jobs
You can begin paving the way for your first full-time job before you ever finish your education by working part-time in a library.

Prior experience is always an added bonus on a resume. Furthermore, getting your foot in the door with a part-time job can lead to a full-time job after graduation.

Internships and Work-Study Programs

You should also look into other options for experience, such as internships and work-study programs. Besides extremely sought-after internships at the Library of Congress and the National Library of Medicine, many research, academic, and special libraries offer internships that can lead to future jobs.

Help on Campus

College placement services can really be helpful in finding a job. They post job listings, and many help with the writing of resumes and send your credentials to prospective employers. Don't overlook studying college bulletin boards and talking to faculty members, fellow students, and alumni when searching for a job.

Job Hot Lines

The phone is your friend when seeking a job. There are a fantastic number of hot lines that have the latest job listings. The American Library Association can give you the numbers of state, regional, and association hot lines. Or look in the classified section of *American Libraries*, the association's magazine.

Internet

Many general online job-search websites post information on library vacancies. Library-related listservs and association and state library agency sites also list job openings.

Classified Ads

Most library journals have classified ad sections that list jobs. You can even advertise your own availability in some of these journals, listing your experience and education plus your preferences—job title, location, salary, and so forth.

Librarian Conventions

Go to the annual conventions of library associations. Many have job placement programs. You can even send your credentials in before some conventions start.

Directories and Employment Guides

The *American Library Directory* lists all kinds of libraries in a two-volume directory. Its only weakness is that some school and special libraries don't return their forms so they aren't listed.

One of the most complete resources with all kinds of hot-line numbers, Internet websites, and addresses is the *Guide to Employment Sources in the Library and Information Professions.* This guide also offers information on job hunting in general and should be looked at by all job seekers. It is available online at the American Library Association website, or you can obtain single copies of this guide by writing to:

Office for Human Resource Development and Recruitment
American Library Association
50 East Huron Street
Chicago, IL 60611
www.ala.org

Federal Government Information

Don't overlook getting a job with the government. To work in many of the federal libraries, you will have to establish civil service eligibility and be placed on the Office of Personnel Management (OPM) register in the geographic area in which you wish to be considered.

Other agencies, such as the FBI, CIA, and Library of Congress, have their own special procedures for hiring. Applicants should contact the agencies directly.

Making a Living as a Librarian

Your salary as a librarian will vary according to your qualifications and the type, size, and location of your workplace. The annual American Library Association survey in 2001 showed a salary range from a low of $20,000 to a high of $274,519, with a mean of $47,852. For all positions, salaries are usually highest in the North Atlantic and West/Southwest regions and lowest in the Southeast. You can get a better idea of what you might make as a librarian by studying the salaries listed in online ads for librarians and in professional journals. The table below shows the mean salaries paid for particular positions in 2000 and 2001.

Title	2001	2000
Directors	$72,384	$70,124
Deputy/Associate/Assistant Directors	$59,346	$57,210
Department Heads/ Coordinators/Senior Managers	$52,677	$50,003
Managers/Supervisors of Support Staff	$42,629	$41,224
Librarians who do not supervise	$42,704	$40,883
Beginning Librarians	$32,891	$32,160

Source: American Library Association Survey of Librarian Salaries, 2001

What Else Can You Do with a Library Degree?

Just because you graduated from college with a librarian's degree is no reason you have to become a librarian. Librarians can use their specialized knowledge in many other satisfying careers requiring similar analytical, organizational, communication, and database skills. Look at this list of book-related and information-related careers many librarians are following:

  researcher
  bookseller
  archivist
  editor
  information consultant
  indexer
  storyteller
  author
  abstractor
  information broker
  records manager
  database specialist
  systems analyst
  book reviewer
  historian
  information systems manager
  museum curator
  publisher's sales representative
  Web master or Web developer

Future Outlook for Librarians

Today, there is an explosion of knowledge both in printed and online material in every field that you can think of. American Library Association President John W. Berry describes current librarians as the human search engines we increasingly count on to help us sort through all this information.

Opportunities abound for librarians, both within and outside the traditional setting of the library. In fact, public libraries and libraries in schools and colleges are now facing or anticipating a shortage of qualified librarians to fill vacancies. And information brokers, private corporations, and consulting firms are all looking for librarians because of their abilities to review, analyze, evaluate, and organize vast amounts of information.

....

For Further Reading

The image of a librarian sitting behind a desk checking books in and out is decidedly not a description of today's librarians. Although this may still be part of the job, librarians have become information specialists adept at using computers to search for written material throughout the world. Learn more about career opportunities for librarians by reading the following career books:

Crawford, Walt. *Being Analog: Creating Tomorrow's Libraries.*
Chicago: American Library Association Editions, 1999.
Gorman, Michael. *Our Enduring Values: Librarianship in the 21st Century.* Chicago: American Library Association Editions, 2000.
Leone, Laura. *Choosing a Career in Information Science.* New York: Rosen Publishing Group, 2001.
McCook, Kathleen de la Peña. *Opportunities in Libraries and Information Science Careers.* Chicago: VGM Career Books, 2002.
Nesbeitt, Sarah L., and Rachel Singer Gordon. *The Information Professional's Guide to Career Development Online.* Medford, NJ: Information Today, 2001.
Shontz, Priscilla K.; Steven J. Oberg; and Robert N. Klob. *JumpStart Your Career in Library and Information Science.* Lanham, MD: Scarecrow Press, 2002.

CHAPTER THREE

Careers in Book Publishing

Bringing New Books to People

Once upon a time authors did it all. They needed no one else to put out a book. An author wrote a book by picking up a stylus to etch the book onto clay tablets. Then the author shared the book with interested readers. Today, with the advent of so much technology, many authors are once again publishing their own books. Most books, however, do not come directly from the author to readers. Hordes of editors, proofreaders, designers, and printers work on books before they ever reach readers' hands. Should you decide to work in the book publishing industry, you could be one of these people.

In the United States there are more than twenty-two hundred major book publishing companies. There are also approximately twenty thousand small or independent publishers. Together, they publish approximately sixty thousand hardcover and paperback books every year and employ more than eighty-one thousand people. A career in this industry can be just right for a confirmed bookworm because so many jobs in book publishing involve considerable reading. There are jobs that let you:

- read manuscripts all day and decide whether they will be published
- edit the author's writing to make it more powerful
- sell books to bookstores and schools

- find typographical errors that a printer has made
- even write your opinion of books

A Glimpse into the Book Publishing Industry

Browse through a bookstore and you will find children's books, travel books, religious books, home improvement books, cookbooks, romance novels, and an amazing number of other kinds of books. Most of these are called trade books, and they make up about one-third of all the books sold. Believe it or not, more books are sold as textbooks for students from kindergarten through college than as trade books for the general public. There is also a market for reference books, such as dictionaries, encyclopedias, and atlases, as well as for scholarly books put out by university presses. Some companies publish a wide variety of books on a broad range of subjects, while others only fill a particular niche.

Just as books come in all sizes, so do publishing companies; however, most are small publishing houses. The largest companies may employ thousands of people, while the smallest may only have two employees—the publisher and an assistant. You are more likely to have a specific job, such as copyeditor or proofreader, at a larger firm; at a smaller firm you could wear several hats at once.

You may find it helpful to know what the usual organization chart looks like in a large publishing company:

Editor in Chief
Executive Editor
Editor—Managing or Acquisitions
Associate Editor
Assistant Editor
Editorial Assistant

Naturally, this chart will look slightly different at each publishing house. Copyeditors can be part of the above hierarchy as assistant or associate editors; however, in large houses they are usually found in a separate department.

. . . .
Where to Start

Starting as an Editorial Assistant

You'll never get bored starting in the publishing industry as an editorial assistant because of the large variety of tasks that you will be required to do. There will be plenty of tedious jobs, such as word processing, filing, verifying facts, and returning unacceptable manuscripts. The good news is that you will probably be able to do quite a bit of reading on the job as soon as you know how the publishing house works.

Much of your reading will center on going through the "slush" pile, which is the accumulation of unsolicited manuscripts that drown most publishers. You will be evaluating the potential of each manuscript. You won't be able to select manuscripts for consideration just because you like them; they will have to fit with what the publishing house prints. For example, a Christian publishing house will not be looking for steamy romance stories.

Starting as a Clerk

Janet Peterson entered the publishing industry as a clerk, moved up to a secretarial position, and then became an editorial administrator/permissions editor. Janet was definitely not a bookworm while she was in school. Today, however, she finds she is reading at least one-third of the time on her job. Janet feels that reading is essential if you plan to grow in a job. She has to keep up with what is happening in the publishing industry and often reads publishing and library journals.

As editorial administrator, Janet is resourceful in managing information and interacting with the education and publishing communities. At times, she has arranged education trade shows and has frequently sat in the booth at shows answering questions about products. In her role as permissions editor, she reviews requests and grants permission to teachers and authors to use information from products published by her employer. Janet also negotiates with authors and publishers for permission to use their materials.

Starting at a Children's Publishing House

Sometimes getting an entry-level job can be based upon who you know. A burned-out schoolteacher found a job as a junior editor at a children's publishing house because she knew someone who worked there. Today, this former teacher is a children's book editor. As an editorial assistant, called "junior editor" at her company, her work was not glamorous. She typed, filed, researched, and learned to edit with the help of an editor. Gradually, she was given books to edit.

First Steps on the Editorial Ladder

After one or two years as an editorial assistant, you will probably begin to move up the editorial ladder. The irony is that the higher you climb, the less time you will be able to devote to reading because so many administrative tasks intervene. Many senior editors find that their job-related reading has become their homework. They do it while they commute, in the evening, on weekends, and on holidays.

Assistant Editor—a Reader's Job

Up one notch from an editorial assistant, the assistant editor at most publishing houses primarily does copyediting and proofreading. At this level, bookworms should be in heaven because there is so much reading to do. Be warned, though, that some assistant editors are weaned away from reading to become more involved with the editorial production of books. This can mean working with the art department or designers on page layout and illustrations.

Copyeditor

Copyeditors usually get manuscripts from editors who have worked on the content and organization. They fix what is still wrong. No two copyeditors have exactly the same job. At some houses, they may do considerable rewriting, while at others they only mark typographical errors. In either case, copyeditors are responsible for checking spelling, grammar, and punctuation. They look for inconsistencies in copy, such as first boarding a plane and later disembarking from a ship (rather than the plane). They also have to find and eliminate repetitions. They read an entire manuscript paragraph by paragraph, line by line, and finally word by word. Many copyeditors now use computers, but some still prefer to use good old-fashioned pencils and write directly on the manuscripts.

A manuscript is always read more than once because copyediting also involves keeping track of the plot and making sure that events fall into the correct slots on a time line. Often the first reading is quick to get the overall idea of the manuscript. The next reading involves marking errors. Corrections are made, then after a final rereading, the manuscript goes back to the author. The author may also make changes, which are copyedited in another reading. The manuscript is checked again when it comes back from the typesetter and every time any changes are made in the copy.

Proofreader

Do you have the eyes of an eagle? Are you good at finding typographical errors on the printed page? Do you have the ability to scrutinize manuscripts closely? Are you a good speller? Even if you answer "yes" to the above questions, you will need to be able to prove your proofreading skills by taking a test that includes a spelling and grammar before you are hired.

Proofreading involves checking that copy from the printer exactly matches the manuscript. To proofreaders, finding inconsistencies is almost like a game. Training is required for this job. Many proofreaders have gone to schools; more have probably learned on the job. Although all copyeditors do some proofreading, freelancers do much of it.

Assistant Editor—Romances

At Harlequin Books, which publishes sixty paperback romance books each month, the entry-level position on the editorial side is assistant editor. To obtain this position, you have to demonstrate the ability to read a book and know if it meets the company's standards, fix a story so it flows, critique a plot, edit text, and write cover copy. Most successful applicants have degrees in English.

Assistant editors at Harlequin begin working under senior editors, who supervise the training. One thing they have to learn is how to write revision letters, which explain changes editors think would improve an author's manuscript. Assistant editors read senior editors' revision letters as part of acquiring this skill. They also read submissions from the "slush" pile to find possible new acquisitions.

Each assistant editor is assigned a stable of authors who regularly write Harlequin books. He or she will edit these books and begin to find his or her own repeat authors from the "slush" pile.

Associate Editor—a Varied Position

After working for a few years as an assistant editor, the next step at many companies is associate editor. It's a good promotion for a reader because it means less clerical work but still with considerable reading. At the same time, of course, the responsibilities increase. This usually means more contact with authors, especially because you have the authority to make more changes in manuscripts. You make rewrite suggestions for cuts and additions and have far more leverage in how a book is edited. In addition, you may begin to become involved in the acquisition of new books.

An Associate Editor

Karen Zack Ingebretsen started working as a proofreader at Time-Life Books ten days after her graduation from college. She willingly skipped the ceremony in order to get a jump on the June crowd of job seekers by interviewing on her commencement day. Karen was required to take a typical proofreading test. After getting the job, Karen, who truly enjoys reading, found out that her job consisted entirely of reading. For forty hours a week, Karen read manuscripts for everything from recipe books to opera librettos in foreign languages that she couldn't speak. In two years, her job disappeared due to a layoff.

Karen then became a production editor/copyeditor at Prentice-Hall. As a production editor, she worked with the art department on concepts for illustrations and covers. She was also responsible for designing interiors, trafficking schedules, and monitoring the flow of manuscript and proof between the typesetter and author. This part of the job only took 25 percent of her time. She spent the rest of the time reading as she edited copy. Once again, Karen lost her job to a layoff.

Karen began to believe that she would never last long enough on a job to get the seniority that was needed to survive a layoff. She considered many alternatives, including teaching English in a foreign country and joining the Peace Corps. However, before she could implement a career change, she acquired a new job at Editing, Design, and Production as a project editor. This job still required Karen to read 75 percent of her time because the company took over the production of books for publishing houses with small staffs. She was doing the same type of work as at her previous job, with the added dimension of keeping the publisher, who was now a client, informed of the progress on a book that she was working on. Marriage brought a move to Chicago, where Karen found a job as an associate editor at a general reference publisher.

Karen was promoted twice at the Chicago firm and became a senior editor. She soon discovered that she was doing less and less hands-on editing as she climbed the editorial ladder; rather, she was supervising the work of others, which is typical throughout the publishing industry. Although she still spent some time reading, a large portion of her time was allotted to planning projects and projecting and tracking project costs. She also spent a good deal of time in meetings. Karen did continue to do both professional reading (journals) as well as reading about current events, which was essential in her work for a general reference publisher. As new books were planned, she had to become an "instant expert" on their subjects through extensive background reading.

A New Opportunity. After several years as a senior editor, Karen returned to Time-Life Books, where her career in publishing had begun. It is common for individuals to change companies as they progress up the publishing career ladder. Karen's new job was as a product manager in the new product development department. Her job was to develop new book series, particularly in the areas of American military history, science, health and fitness, popular culture, arts, and cooking. Here her passion for books really came in handy. In order to develop series that would sell well, she had to know what people were reading and what they'd like to be reading. Karen also had to stay versed in publishing trends and in consumer purchasing in general so the company could make sure its material was in sync with or ahead of those trends. This was an exciting job for a bookworm, as she had the opportunity to directly influence the development of the product line.

Unfortunately, Karen's job ended when her department was closed; the parent company was later dissolved. Since then she has been freelancing as a writer and editor for print and electronic publishers. She still makes a point of reading periodicals regularly, as she needs to know about everything under the sun as a freelancer. Karen's career path clearly shows the diversity of jobs in the publishing industry that will give bookworms many opportunities to read for pay.

Editor—Managing or Acquisitions

What an editor does varies greatly from company to company. Some publishing houses have separate positions for managing and acquisitions editors. At other houses, an editor is both a managing and an acquisitions editor. How much editors read truly depends on what their responsibilities are. Some still do quite a lot of reading at their offices, while others spend most of the time working on the business side of publishing.

Managing Editor

These editors are in charge of day-to-day operations. They see that schedules are maintained and supervise junior editors. Managing editors typically oversee the work of the copyeditors, proofreaders, and, in many cases, the designers and illustrators, who are responsible for the way books look.

Acquisitions Editor

These are the editors who have lunches with authors, go to book signings, and attend book fairs. They have the task of bringing in and signing up new books and authors and working with literary agents. They are also supposed to come up with new book ideas.

Editor at a Trade Book Company

The editorial assistant who was described earlier worked her way up the ladder to become an editor of children's books. In this job, she wears the hats of both a managing and an acquisitions editor.

Every fourth week, she becomes an acquisitions editor and goes through as many as seventy-five books in a week. Not all of the seventy-five books are read cover to cover. However, after careful scanning and skimming, each book is placed in a pile indicating its future. This editor clearly knows what she likes and what her company is looking for. She discusses her acquisition choices with other editors. If the majority approves a book, it is sent to the marketing department for a "yes" or "no" vote.

While wearing the hat of managing editor, this editor oversees the production of as many as twenty books in a year. Not only does she decide on text changes, she also acts as a copyeditor, which is something not all editors do.

In describing the pluses and minuses of her job, this editor points out that the job is not dull or routine. Because the subject matter varies greatly, the opportunity to learn something new is always there. The one negative to her job is the tension she feels when she falls behind on her schedule.

Executive Editor

A large publishing house may have an executive editor who oversees the assistant and associate editors and handles many responsibilities typically given to the editor in chief. Executive editors often direct the overall planning and editorial content of the company's publications. They spend time coordinating art, text, prepress, and manufacturing to ensure proper control over production schedules, implementation of technology, quality, and cost. In addition, they may develop long-range plans and monitor developments in the publishing industry to assess the far-reaching implications of trends for their companies.

Executive Editor at World Book

For more than thirty-five years, Dale Jacobs has been at World Book, the publishers of encyclopedias, Childcraft books, and other reference materials for home and school. Dale's career has truly been a bookworm's delight. He describes his first job as an assistant editor at World Book as a reading job with lots of writing, too. Dale read books, periodicals, and leading newspapers to get information for revising encyclopedia articles; he also read and revised contributors' articles. Although all of his jobs have involved considerable reading, Dale did the most reading when he was the social sciences editor and had to keep abreast of what was happening in this field.

As executive editor, a position he held before becoming editor in chief, he often spent half of his day reading memos, correspondence, original and edited manuscripts, and other revision proposals. He also spent a portion of his day doing background reading in the *Wall Street Journal*, the *New York Times*, *Time*, *Newsweek*, and other periodicals related to the creative and business sides of publishing. Dale says that bookworms will have a head start in finding a job with World Book because the company is looking for employees who have read widely to keep up-to-date with current events.

Editor in Chief

At the top of the editorial ladder is the editor in chief, who has almost always climbed the ladder rung by rung to reach this position. This job requires great involvement in the business side of publishing books. The editor in chief makes major decisions on budgeting, scheduling, acquisitions, and marketing strategies. Time is also spent on developing ideas for new books and monitoring the progress of projects. Only a very limited amount of time is spent reading and editing manuscripts.

Editorial Director at Globe Pequot Press

Mike Urban has been in the publishing industry since he left college. To get his first job as an editorial assistant for a publisher of medical journals, he actually had to take a typing test. Although half of his time on this job was spent doing clerical work, the other half was devoted to learning editorial skills, such as copyediting, proofreading, and page layout. After a year, Mike moved to Rand

McNally to work as a research assistant updating listings in travel guides. In this job, as well as in positions as assistant and associate editor, Mike did tons of reading and some writing of travel literature. A move to World Book to become a project editor and later a senior editor gave Mike experience in production tasks. This job also involved considerable reading and research. His next job, however, with NTC Publishing Group as acquisitions editor, gave Mike the perfect job for bookworms: he was reading all the time as he reviewed new and unsolicited manuscripts.

Today, Mike is editorial director at Globe Pequot, a trade travel publisher. Now at the top of the editorial ladder, Mike is doing less reading and concentrating more on administrative tasks. He is in charge of the manufacture and production of 250 new and revised books each year. Plus, he is participating in electronic publishing initiatives. Mike says publishing books involves a lot of tedious work, but when he holds a new book in his hands and knows that he played a role in its creation, he feels rewarded.

Publisher or President

At many publishing houses, there is a publisher or president at the top directing the entire operation. Although publishers tend to be bookworms, this is not a hands-on manuscript job. It involves supervising every department of the company. This job involves a lot of reading, but it is in the form of memos, financial statements, and professional journals.

President of Free Spirit Publishing

Not all publishing companies are large. In the early days of Free Spirit Publishing, Judy Galbraith was author, editor, business manager, and office manager. Today, the company has a staff of twenty-eight full-time employees, including a vice president, a sales manager, a production manager, two in-house production designers, and three in-house editors who work with freelance editors. There are also other employees doing various jobs from order processing and shipping to customer assistance and editorial research.

Not all publishers rise through the editorial ranks to achieve their positions. Judy Galbraith was a teacher who started Free Spirit Publishing after purchasing the publishing rights to her first book, which had been published by another publisher. The company has grown steadily and has published 125 titles since its inception in 1983. Judy loves to read but is compelled to devote her office hours to the publishing business. However, at home, after work, and on weekends and airplanes, she spends hours reading trade publications and manuscripts.

· · · · · · · · · · · · · · · ·

Indexer

If you like the idea of doing freelance work in the publishing industry, indexing is an excellent job possibility because few companies have full-time indexers on staff. Furthermore, some publishing houses leave indexing up to authors, who, in turn, usually look for freelance indexers to do this work.

In creating an index, an indexer makes an alphabetical list of a book's contents and lists page numbers where each item is discussed. Here is a job where a bookworm is being paid to read a book. Although books on every subject from podiatry to forestry are indexed, you will need some experience in a subject to index a book. Most indexers have advanced degrees and specialize in certain subjects. The job also requires organizational skills and the ability to determine what is important in a book. Computer skills are a must because indexing has gone high tech. Doing indexes on three-by-five cards is a thing of the past. In addition, indexers must be able to function well under pressure. Indexing is always a rush job because indexers are the last in line to get copy.

Acquiring Indexing Skills

You need some training to become an indexer. A publisher is going to expect you to have specific knowledge about indexing.

Unfortunately, there are few indexing classes. Some can be found at colleges that have schools of library science. The United States Department of Agriculture (USDA) offers two correspondence courses. For further information about these courses, go online to the USDA website or write to:

Graduate School, USDA
Correspondence Study Program
South Agriculture Building, Room 1112
1400 Independence Avenue SW
Washington, DC 20250
www.usda.gov/programs_services/corres/cop.cfm

The National Federation of Abstracting and Information Services (NFAIS) offers seminars in indexing that can help both beginning and experienced indexers. This organization also publishes the *Career Guide to Careers in Indexing and Abstracting*, which is available for a fee. Contact this organization through its website or by writing to:

NFAIS
1518 Walnut Street, Suite 307
Philadelphia, PA 19102
www.nfais.org

The indexing field is a small one. Many indexers belong to the American Society of Indexers. Through membership in this organization, indexers get newsletters, other publications at a discount, subscriptions to *The Indexer: Journal of the Society Indexers* and *Key Words: The Bulletin of the American Society of Indexers,* a discount on conference fees, plus the opportunity to talk with other indexers at local organizations of the society. Information about this organization can be obtained by visiting its website or writing to:

American Society of Indexers
10200 West Forty-Fourth Avenue, Suite 304
Wheat Ridge, CO 80033
www.asindexing.org

Working as an Indexer

You can make a living as a freelance indexer. Although what you are paid will vary from area to area, an experienced indexer averages about $30 an hour. You will earn more if you are very fast or handle very complicated material. The most common method of billing is charging for each indexable page (typically, $3 per page and up to $10 per page for complicated manuscripts). You get a job as an indexer through contacts with editors and other indexers and by sending resumes to publishing companies. In addition, new employment opportunities for indexers are available making indexes of online materials and CD-ROMs.

An Indexer at World Book

David Pofelski feels lucky to work at a company as an indexer. There are not many of these jobs. After college, he had no idea what he would like to do, except he felt publishing was an intriguing area. He found his job at Encyclopaedia Britannica as an indexer and has remained in this field throughout most of his career. He spent nine years at home working as a freelancer doing his indexing on index cards before purchasing a computer. David has been at World Book since 1988. At first, his indexing work was primarily of printed materials. Now, much of what he indexes is online materials.

Indexing has become far more mechanized in the past twenty years. Indexers no longer have to worry so much about clerical details and are freer to concentrate on the quality of what they are producing. The advent of the computer has also cut the number of indexers required on David's company's staff.

David enjoys his job because he likes to read and especially likes reading a variety of materials and learning so much about different subjects. He approaches indexing as a craft and tries to do the best possible job on each index. The job has some negative aspects. He spends his entire day looking at a terminal, and there is considerable clerical work keying words in and checking for accuracy. He also works under tremendous pressure to get jobs done.

....

Literary Agent

Just because an author writes a book doesn't mean you'll ever be able to find it on a library shelf. It isn't easy for an author to get a book published, especially because many publishing companies won't even look at a manuscript unless a literary agent submits it. In this country, there are more than three hundred literary agencies. Whether an agency is run by one person or has hundreds of employees, the dream is to find the next bestseller.

Literary agents represent authors to publishers, and they also act as negotiators between the two. Today, due to time restraints, more publishers are relying on literary agents to produce new authors and materials.

Literary agents' days are never routine. They always buzz with activity. A typical day may include working with authors, editors, lawyers, and accountants. Agents may suggest changes to an author that will make a book marketable, mediate a conflict between an author and an editor, as well as boost the flagging spirits of yet another author. They may try to convince an editor that an author in the agency's stable has just written a novel that will become an American classic—or at least sell more than ten thousand copies. The agents may wheel and deal with lawyers to get the best contract for a first-time author. They may check recent sales figures with an accountant. More than likely, they will also suffer rejection. Some books that they absolutely love will never be sold to a publisher. Others may take years to sell. Rejection, even frequent rejection, is an accepted part of a literary agent's job.

Between all the paperwork and the never-ending phone calls, literary agents do not have a lot of time for reading during office hours. Yet reading is an important part of a literary agent's work; it is the only way to discover books to sell to editors. So reading time must be snatched whenever possible at the office, but most of it is done after hours.

You don't just set up shop as a literary agent. Most literary agents are former editors who have an eye for manuscripts that will sell. They can read the first thirty pages of a manuscript or the proposal for a book and know right away whether or not it has possibilities. Besides being able to recognize a saleable manuscript, a literary agent is really a jack-of-all-trades who has the ability to

- handle people effectively
- shape an author's career
- know where different manuscripts can be sold
- negotiate contracts
- help authors edit their manuscripts

Bookworms can enjoy even an entry-level position as an assistant in a literary agency. The job involves many of the same duties as an editorial assistant. However, because many of the agencies are small, an assistant at an agency does more reading than in a large publishing house. The job could include reading manuscripts and writing reviews; typing and filing correspondence to authors and publishers; and scheduling meetings among authors, agents, and publishers. Some assistants become full-fledged agents or editors at publishing firms, while a few start their own agencies.

Book Reviewer

Imagine getting a free copy of a book and then being paid to read it. That's what happens when you are a book reviewer. Because the job is so appealing, there are a great number of book reviewers. Unfortunately, only a few of them are able to make a living at this job. For that reason, freelancers usually do book reviewing for publication.

Book reviewers are normally paid for each review. How much you receive for a review depends on the size of the newspaper or magazine, the length and complexity of the review, and, occasionally, on your reputation as a reviewer. You could receive nothing except a new book or as much as $500. By selling the same review to different markets in geographically separated areas or in shorter or longer versions, it is possible to increase your income. You might be able to make as much as $1,000 for a single review.

To become a book reviewer, you need to be more than an avid reader; you also have to have writing ability. You can learn how to be an expert book reviewer by studying book reviews that others have written and by taking courses. Just working in the publishing industry will also give you some of the experience you need.

Reading a book is the easiest part of being a book reviewer. The hardest is finding someone who wants you to write a review. Dave Wood, former book editor of the *Minneapolis Star Tribune*, had the names of 250 book reviewers in his file. During a typical year, less than half of these reviewers would actually write reviews for the newspaper. Only fifty to sixty were asked frequently to write reviews.

The road to being one of the lucky people chosen to write a review is a rough one. What you have to do is send a resume and samples of your work to newspapers and magazines. This frequently accomplishes nothing more than getting your name in a Rolodex file. You can also send unsolicited reviews. If an editor is looking for the book you reviewed, you may be on your way to becoming paid for reviewing books.

Book reviewers with some experience, even if it is for a small newspaper or magazine, can join the National Book Critics Circle. Members' names, along with their specialties, are put into a directory that book editors use to find reviewers. The organization also publishes a newsletter and offers regional and national seminars that provide helpful information for book reviewers. You can join the National Book Critics Circle if you write a minimum of three book reviews a year and pay a fee. For information, visit the organization's website or contact:

Vice President/Membership
Bloomsbury Review, English Department
Rockland Community College
145 College Road
Suffern, NY 10901
www.bookforum.com/bloomsbury

Reviewing Books for a Magazine

One of the first places in which books are reviewed is *Publishers Weekly.* Valiska Gregory reviews four to six children's books each month for this magazine. Usually, the books are so new that she is reading from color proofs that are not even bound together.

When she reviews a children's book, Valiska tries to assess the author's purpose from the text and illustrations. She always reads a book more than once. She doesn't follow any particular format in writing her reviews, but she does try to indicate what the book is about as well as assess the book's literary and artistic merit. She often compares a book to similar ones.

Valiska, who is an author and poet as well as a freelance book reviewer, obtained her reviewing job through personal contacts. While attending a publishing course, she met a woman who became an editor of *Publishers Weekly.*

Reviewing Books for a Newspaper

Working in the library at a newspaper gave Betsy Caulfield the opportunity to meet the book editor and led to her becoming a freelance book reviewer. As a dedicated bookworm, Betsy always read book reviews. She got the idea of becoming a reviewer because she frequently disagreed with reviewers of books that she had read and wanted to share her opinion with others. She now reviews about one book each month after reading the entire book to get its essence.

· ·

Selecting Books for Book Clubs

Every few weeks, millions of homes, especially the homes of bookworms, receive selection magazines from book clubs. Besides the well-known Book-of-the-Month Club and Literary Guild, there are specific clubs that cater to interests ranging from cooking, astronomy, and religion to photography, farming, and ecology. Children's books are offered through many of these clubs as well as separate children's clubs. Each club typically offers the opportunity to purchase new selections along with backlist titles.

Like the climber who reaches the top of Mount Everest, a bookworm who becomes a selector for a book club has reached the summit of his or her dreams. This job involves reading books and then deciding which should be offered to members. At some clubs, all the selectors are in-house editors reading literally from nine to five. At other houses, the editors do most of their reading at home while attending to marketing and administrative chores on the job. Most houses also use freelance selectors, who do a first reading and are typically paid between $50 and $100 per manuscript.

Bookworms who become selectors usually have bachelor's degrees behind their names. Their degrees certainly don't have to be in English but usually are in some area of liberal arts. It is possible to get a job as a selector right after graduating from college. However, many get this job after working as administrative assistants, copyeditors, or at some other job in publishing. Don't bother applying for this job unless you are a speed-reader. You should be able to read a thousand pages in twelve to fifteen hours.

Working as a Book Selector

"Sometimes, the pages just turned themselves," according to Jaye Isler, who was an editorial assistant at a major book club. At other times, she didn't even complete a book because it wasn't right for the book club's members. Jaye, like other selectors, is a confirmed book lover. She confesses that she would far rather meet an author than a Hollywood star.

Jaye's job as an editorial assistant was a busy one with long hours. She didn't usually read manuscripts at the office but was involved in such things as making sure that books that were to be listed in the club's magazine were in stock and that there were pictures of these books. She also checked that the copy describing the books was accurate. At any given time, she was working on book information that would go in any one of eight selection magazines. In addition, she spent considerable time in meetings and negotiating with publishers to obtain the rights to a book.

Outside the office, Jaye read for approximately ten hours a week. During that time, she would read two or three books to determine whether the club should offer them to its members. When selectors begin working at Jaye's book club, they learn how to do the job by reading book evaluations that experienced selectors have made. At first, their evaluations are checked to make sure they understand what the club is looking for. "The longer one selects books for a club," Jaye says, "the easier it becomes to tell which books will satisfy the club members." Today, Jaye is spending much of her time writing; however, she still spends some time reading and making selections for the book club.

Owning Your Own Bookstore

To a bookworm, owning a bookstore must seem like the best of all possible worlds. You can choose the books that you want for the store and look at new books before they are even bound.

Owning a Children's Bookstore

Before Shirley Mullin became a bookstore owner, she was a teacher. Now she owns two children's bookstores, called Kids Ink. Bookstore owners get to do a lot of job-related reading. Shirley sees most new children's books from six to nine months before they are published. When she first sees a book, she is usually not looking at the finished copy but at galleys for the book. She reads all the children's picture books herself but doesn't have time to read all the other books, so she farms some of them out to her staff. Shirley often reads reviews, which usually come out after she has read the galleys for new books. By reading the reviews, she can see if she has missed any promising new books or if she wishes to reexamine any books that she has read. Shirley is helped in her selection process by knowledgeable publishing company representatives and her own staff.

Working at a Retail Bookstore

Along with libraries, bookstores seem the perfect habitat for bookworms. And there are twenty-five thousand retail bookstores as possible workplaces, ranging from small, specialized shops to superstores. In a bookstore, surrounded by books, a bookworm may not have too much opportunity to read on the job. However, bookstore employees are encouraged to read book reviews and books so that they can help customers find the books they want. At many stores, the owners and managers also want employee input on what books should be added to a store's stock. An added dividend for bookstore employees can be purchasing books for a discounted price.

Part of the recent strong growth in sales of trade books is because of the emergence of book superstores. Many cities now have at least one book superstore, which has contributed to the growth in sales of trade books. These stores stock from thirty thousand to eighty thousand titles. The managers of these stores are actively searching for bookworms who really know books—from popular bestsellers to less-well-known offerings from small publishing houses.

More Jobs Associated with Books

The more you learn about all the steps involved in bringing a book from author to reader, the more you'll know about the great variety of jobs that will actually let you read books. Taking an entry-level job or an internship are two ways many bookworms have become acquainted with interesting jobs like the following.

Designing Books

Someone has to decide just what a finished book is going to look like so it will appeal to readers. All the artwork, the headings, and the arrangement of the material on the pages have to be related to what is said on the pages. Each book needs to have a design theme. A job working in this area can tie your interest in books with an artistic background.

Illustrating Books

Illustrations are an important part of many books and must tie closely to the text. In order to do this successfully, the illustrator needs to carefully read the manuscript. Children's books and textbooks are usually full of illustrations. At times, illustrating is done in-house, but more often freelance illustrators do it.

Selling Books

For a bookworm, it's a lot more enjoyable to sell books than to sell aluminum siding or automobiles. Working as a sales representative for a publisher or distributor not only gives you the chance to read many of the books that you are trying to sell, you also get to talk about them to bookstore owners, buyers for chains, and librarians. If you are selling textbooks, you will talk to both teachers and selection committees. No matter where you are selling books, your commission will be based on how well you know the product—books. Being a sales representative is a great career for a bookworm because the more you read, the more you earn, and you will get the added benefit of traveling.

In this position, everyone learns on the job. The better you sell, the better your territory will be. Success in sales can also lead to management job offers in the home office. Some sales representatives even branch off on their own and become independent sales representatives.

More Career Possibilities

Even more career opportunities exist in book publishing for bookworms. Besides the many careers that have been mentioned, you may want to investigate some of the following career areas:

marketing
promotion
publicity
corporate administration
advertising
production
public relations

You won't just find jobs with publishers. Book jobbers and distributors, direct- and subscription-mail sales organizations, and bookstore chains are other areas where bookworms can find jobs that let them be close to books in some way.

Earning a Living in the Book Business

The book publishing industry is definitely not a get-rich-quick place to work. Entry-level employees are not highly paid relative to their education levels. Editorial assistants average $30,700 a year. Editors average $57,000 a year, and editors in chief average $112,000, according to a 2001 survey in *Publishers Weekly*.

Furthermore, because most of the book publishing industry is centered in New York and Chicago, your climb up the ladder will involve paying a premium price for your living quarters. Remembering that your salary should increase a little with each rung of the ladder and that you are working with books should help bookworms overcome the negatives of careers in book publishing.

Preparing for a Career in Book Publishing

Working in book publishing may not always be well paid, but it is an exciting field that many college graduates want to enter. There is strong competition for entry-level jobs, especially at major publishing houses. You will need a college degree. You will also need to excel in your use of the English language. A strong computer background that includes keyboarding and editing abilities is important.

Getting experience by working with books in some capacity will make you a stronger candidate for a job. Working part-time in a bookstore or library can be helpful. Finding a part-time job with a publishing house is even better because you can then show actual work experience in the industry. Working as an intern at a publishing company will also strengthen your resume. Both part-time jobs and internships can lead to job offers because they let publishing companies become acquainted with your work. You can find out what internships are available by looking at directories listing internships. You will find these directories in the reference section of the library.

Attending book publishing courses, conferences, workshops, and seminars will increase your insight into what the industry is like. Reading *Publishers Weekly* will let you know what is happening in publishing. It has a calendar that gives current information on courses, workshops, and seminars; there is even a jobs section in the magazine. It is also smart to become acquainted with the

Literary Market Place (LMP), available in most library reference sections. This directory lists the names, addresses, and phone numbers of book publishers in the United States and Canada. The publishers are even classified by subject matter. You will also find information about book courses, conferences, and events. There are lists of literary agents, book clubs, and foreign publishers as well as information about acquisitions and mergers in the industry. A lot of information is available on the website at www.literarymarketplace.com.

A Glimpse into the Future

The demand for books should grow in the next five years as the population increases in the book-buying age group. More textbooks and school library books will be needed as school enrollment increases. And as the middle-aged and older populations expand, so will the demand for more leisure reading materials. In addition, the foreign market for books is growing. As the demand for books increases, the need for employees, especially in editorial, marketing, and administrative positions, should increase. New opportunities for bookworms will emerge in the area of nonprint formats for books, including audio books and CD-ROM discs.

For Further Reading

Isn't it ironic that one of the best ways to prepare for a career in book publishing is by reading to learn all you can about the industry? As Lord Chesterfield once wrote, "The best companions are the best books." The following books should become your companions if you are serious about learning more about a career in book publishing.

Einsohn, Amy, and Marc Einsohn. *The Copyeditor's Handbook: A Guide for Book Publishing and Corporate Communications with Exercises and Answer Keys.* Berkeley, CA: University of California Press, 2000.

Herman, Jeff. *Writer's Guide to Book Editors, Publishers, and Literary Agents, 2002–2003: Who They Are! What They Want! And How to Win Them Over!* Rocklin, CA: Prima Publishing, 2001.

Literary Market Place—The Directory of American Book Publishing. New York: R. R. Bowker Company (annual).

Oakes, Meredith. *The Editing Process.* London: Oberon, 1998.

Pattis, S. William, and Robert A. Carter. *Opportunities in Publishing Careers.* Chicago: VGM Career Books, 2000.

Rooney, Edmond, and Oliver Witte. *Copy Editing for Professionals.* Champaign, IL: Stipes Publishing Company, 2000.

Ryan, Buck; Michael O'Donnell; and Leland B. Ryan. *The Editor's Toolbox: A Reference Guide for Beginners and Professionals.* Ames, IA: Iowa State University Press, 2001.

CHAPTER FOUR

Careers with Magazines and Newspapers

Providing Information for Readers

While riding on buses and trains, eating solitary meals in restaurants, or relaxing in the sun, bookworms who don't have their noses in books are likely to be reading magazines and newspapers. They typically delve into these popular printed materials to keep informed about what is happening in the world, and so do many other people, thus creating many jobs that are appealing to bookworms.

There were newspapers before there were magazines. In fact, magazines actually developed from newspapers. The original reason for having magazines was to review books, while newspapers concentrated more on news. Both early magazines and newspapers looked much the same and were held together by folds. The difference was that newspapers had numerous folds, while magazines only had one. Because magazines fell apart easily, they were soon bound.

While today some magazines and newspapers still may look the same, most magazines differ in these obvious ways:

higher grade of paper
distinctive cover
more varied typeface

more color illustrations
different writing style
more white space

Both newspapers and magazines have many jobs that require considerable reading. By finding out more about what jobs are available at each of these publications, bookworms can decide which is a better career fit for their personalities.

A Closer Look at Magazines

Publications bound in paper covers that appear regularly and contain stories, articles, and illustrations by various contributors are usually called magazines. Magazines are also called periodicals, publications, journals, reviews, newsletters, and even books. So, whenever you see one of these words in a want ad, you may be looking at an advertisement for a job on a magazine.

Join the staff of a magazine, and you are joining a long list of literary greats. Throughout the history of magazines, many well-known authors worked on magazine staffs, contributed articles to magazines, and even started magazines. Charles Dickens, Washington Irving, Oliver Wendell Holmes, Ralph Waldo Emerson, and Henry Adams were all involved in some way with magazines.

New Media Have Not Vanquished Magazines

Neither movies, television, nor videos have grabbed such a giant share of people's attention that magazines are no longer being read. In fact, today, more than 17,500 different magazines are being published in the United States. Furthermore, each year several hundred new magazines are started. In 2000, nearly 350 new magazines were launched. Admittedly, it is a tough market to crack because only a handful last. Benjamin Franklin couldn't make it with his *General Magazine*. But in spite of all the competition, some magazines, such as *People*, do succeed quite sensationally. Still, many prominent old magazines have folded. The sale of magazines continues to be strong. In 2000, nearly four hundred million magazines were sold in the United States. With more than 126,000 people employed in the publishing of these magazines, this is a good place for bookworms to look for jobs that involve reading.

Finding the Right Magazine

Just walk into any drugstore, bookstore, or even the grocery store and check out the magazine racks. It won't take longer than a few minutes to discover that there are magazines on almost any subject that you can think of, from coin collecting to family health. Most of these fall into the category of consumer magazines. The other large category is business publications, which are trade, technical, and professional magazines. There are jobs for bookworms in both categories.

Consumer Magazines

More than eight thousand different consumer magazines are sold in the United States. Their circulations and revenues far exceed those of the greater number of trade, technical, and professional magazines. Only a small number of consumer magazines deal with general interests; most are devoted to specialized topics. Job seekers who want to work on magazines appealing to general interests usually have degrees in journalism or English. Obtaining a job on magazines with very large circulations can be quite competitive. Experience will count in getting one of these jobs.

On the other hand, if you want to work for a specialized consumer magazine, such as one dealing with computers, needlework, motorcycles, crafts, dancing, or antiques, you definitely need some knowledge or experience in that area. You are not going to get a job at a specialized computer magazine—an area that has nearly seven hundred magazines—unless you know what bytes, bits, crashing, and control keys are. Nor will you be a good candidate for a job with a motorcycle magazine if you have never put on a helmet and ridden on a motorcycle. Still, being a bookworm can help you get a job with a specialized magazine if you have done in-depth reading in the area it covers. You can find lists of all the consumer magazines that are currently being published by looking at *National Directory of Magazines* or *SRDS* (Standard Rate and Data Service) *Consumer Magazine Directory.*

Trade, Technical, and Professional Magazines

You won't usually find trade, technical, and professional magazines on magazine racks. You might find one in a doctor's, lawyer's, or accountant's office because many of these publications deal with professions. Just think of any profession; there is probably one or more magazines dealing exclusively with that field. The medical profession has an impressive list of about 960 magazines.

What do you think *Bank News, Boating Industry International, Modern Tire Dealer*, and *Nuclear News* magazines have in common? They bring information to people who are interested in what is happening in these industries. Scarcely an industry in the United States does not have a magazine. Advertising, tobacco, welding, railroads, textiles, travel, sewage disposal, coal mining, bicycles, and luggage all have magazines, to name just a few industries. If you are interested in a career in business magazines, make sure you look at the *SRDS Business Magazine Directory* for a list of all the business magazines that are published. Several large companies publish more than one magazine—some publish as many as forty magazines.

To work on certain trade, technical, and professional magazines, you need academic training in a specific area. People working on medical magazines need to have a scientific or health care background. In other areas, it helps to be knowledgeable about a particular profession or industry; but it is not always essential. You can learn about the field through on-the-job training. Fortunately, bookworms are willing to learn through reading.

....

Editorial Jobs with Magazines

Employees on the editorial side do a lot of reading. Perhaps, the better workplace for a bookworm is a consumer magazine or a magazine for a particular profession. More reading will occur at these magazines because most of the material is being written by outside authors or people within a profession. This means that articles and stories will have to be considered for acquisition and copyedited—both jobs that require considerable reading. If you work for a business magazine that publishes information about an industry, it is likely that you will be doing more writing than reading because many of these magazines are mainly written in-house.

The size of the magazine determines the kind of job you are going to have. If you work for one of the giants in the magazine industry, your job will simply be in one specific area. Work for a magazine with a staff of thirty or forty people, and your job description will be considerably broader. If you really want to be a jack-of-all-trades, get a job on a magazine that has an editorial staff of only one or two people.

The Pecking Order on a Magazine Staff

There really is not much difference between the organization charts of book publishing companies and most magazine publishers. The size of the magazine dictates how many different rungs the editorial ladder will have. What an employee does at any particular job varies from one magazine to another.

Editor in Chief or Editor. Standing on the top rung of the ladder is the editor in chief, who is responsible for the editorial content of the magazine. A person in this position must delegate many responsibilities to other members of the staff.

Managing Editor. Reporting directly to the editor in chief, a managing editor supervises daily activities at the magazine. The managing editor's job also entails handling the staff and freelance writers, as well as writing and editing personal projects. The larger the magazine, the greater the number of assistant editors reporting to the managing editor. Most managing editors rise through the editorial ranks.

Senior, Associate, and Specialty Editors. Depending on the size and organization of a magazine, you will find senior editors, associate editors, copyeditors, and assistant editors. Many of these editors are specialists in certain fields—such as fashion, travel, or politics—and may be called fashion editor, travel editor, political editor, and so forth. All of these editors do some reading; however, out of this group, the copyeditor is the one doing the most reading.

Editorial Assistant. Editorial assistant is an entry-level position in which you not only learn about how a magazine is put out but also how to handle various tasks, from copyediting to acquisition.

Starting at the Bottom of the Ladder

With a recent degree in journalism in hand, Leigh Davis started her career working as an editorial assistant at the *Saturday Evening Post*. She regards this job as a great beginning for an eager bookworm. Leigh feels that it is difficult to get a job in magazine publishing and that more than a degree is needed. She has found that experience counts and thinks that her work on the college newspaper really helped her get this job. Even having worked on a high school newspaper staff would be helpful experience on a job seeker's resume.

Leigh's beginning job on the editorial side required a lot of reading. First of all, she spent a brief period of time every day reading through other general magazines to see what trends these magazines were following, especially in their travel sections.

Approximately one-third of Leigh's day was spent reading and researching as a fact checker. For example, after checking the facts on a travel story on South Padre Island, she researched for general information on other barrier islands. Then she added some of these facts to the travel story.

Another job that took a considerable portion of Leigh's time was reading unsolicited manuscripts. A select few were forwarded to editors as possibilities for later publication.

Copyediting, however, is what took up most of Leigh's time in this job. Not only did she have to read and proofread entire articles, she even had to do quite a bit of rewriting on them. What was left of Leigh's day was spent doing clerical tasks, such as sending manuscript guidelines to freelance authors and responding to authors' questions about where their manuscripts were. Because the staff at the *Saturday Evening Post* was quite small, Leigh had the opportunity to work in several different areas, something she feels she would not have been able to do at a larger magazine.

Letters Department Manager

Other jobs on magazine staffs require considerable reading. Ken Porter, manager of the letters department at a national news magazine, has one of those jobs. Roughly a thousand letters arrive by E-mail or fax at this very popular publication each week. Ken and his staff have the responsibility of handling these letters. The letters first go to a clerk who determines where they will be routed. Some are forwarded to other departments. The remaining letters are distributed to the staff of the letters department for reply. Staff members—many with master's degrees in journalism—answer some of these letters.

A great number of the letters are routine and can be answered by form letters or slightly adapted form letters. Others require original replies, often necessitating some research. These letters must be accurate because they reflect the views of the editors of the news magazine. The letters correspondents often need to consult with the author of an article for help in drafting a reply.

Each week, one of the staff members sorts through all the letters and divides them into groups that reflect the stories they are commenting on and the viewpoints of the letter writers. Then Ken and some of his staff select the letters to be used in the letters column. Many letters have to be edited for reasons of clarity and space. Ken also adds editor's comments when necessary.

Ken believes that reading letters is an excellent way to start at this news magazine. Not only does this job have the fringe benefit that you might be noticed, it also provides valuable experience in editing, researching, and writing—skills essential to journalism. Ken started in the entry-level position of letter correspondent and is now the manager of the letters department. Before getting his first job in this department, it was necessary for Ken to pass a test demonstrating his ability to write clear conversational prose.

The Magazine Pay Scale

Starting out on the editorial side of the magazine industry will give you much the same income as starting in the book publishing industry. Most entry-level positions average slightly more than $20,000 a year. At all levels, you will make more working for trade, technical, and professional magazines than at consumer magazines. You will also make more money at magazines with larger circulations. If you are working on a magazine in the Northeast, you will earn more than in any other region. It is also quite likely that you will be working in the area around New York City because that is the hub of the magazine industry. Unfortunately, it also costs more to live in this region.

Getting Your Foot in the Door

No one, perfect route guarantees a job with a magazine. Certainly, a liberal arts degree seems to be a starting point for most people working on the editorial side of magazine publishing. Experience with a publication—from high school newspaper to college literary magazine—is also helpful. Even a little experience lets a prospective magazine employee write down something in the spaces asking for experience on application forms.

Having an internship on a magazine is an excellent way to get the experience job hunters need. Some internships are part-time jobs during the school year in which students receive academic credit and no money. There are also summer programs that offer some pay. You will find that most publishers have intern programs for undergraduates and recent graduates.

The reference section of the library has many directories listing internships. Before you sign up for an internship program, make sure that it is project oriented and that you know exactly what you will be doing. Twelve weeks of meaningless clerical work could seem like an eternity. It can also be helpful to select an internship at a firm where you would later like to work. Another avenue in preparing for a job in magazine publishing is attending a writing course during the summer.

The First Steps as an Intern

Jennie Duffy, a recent college graduate in communications, wants to find a job on a weekly lifestyle magazine. She needs solid recommendations from an employer in this area, experience in working on a magazine, and samples of her work to show prospective employers. Jennie hopes to fill these needs through a three-month internship with Diablo Publications, working on the firm's *Diablo* magazine, a lifestyle magazine in Northern California. As an intern, she has been able to do some writing and is spending time researching and fact checking. Because the internship only pays a modest stipend, Jennie has two other jobs in order to support herself. Nevertheless, Jennie is optimistic that she is on the way to a career with a magazine.

Your Future in the Magazine Industry

The magazine industry is expected to grow an impressive 11 percent before 2010. This is certainly good news for bookworms seeking jobs in this area. Much of the growth will be in professional, scientific, and technical journals as well as special-interest publications, especially health and physical fitness magazines.

Expect also many new magazines in areas geared to families, teenagers, sports lovers, and other hobbyists. These narrowly targeted magazines will be looking for individuals who can produce a high-quality product. Also, the demand for technical writers is expected to increase because of the ongoing expansion of scientific and technical information and the continued need to communicate it in a readable style in magazines directed at a variety of audiences.

A Closer Look at Newspapers

The first printed newspaper, the *Dibao*, was published during the eighth century in China. Even earlier, newspapers were hand written and posted in public places. One of these was the *Acta Diurna*, meaning *daily events,* which actually started in Rome in 59 B.C.

Benjamin Harris of Boston founded the first newspaper in the United States in 1690. It was called the *Publick Occurrences Both Forreign and Domestick* and had an extraordinarily brief history because the government stopped it after the first issue. The 1800s were the heyday for the development of newspapers. The largest number of newspapers ever in the United States was about twenty-six hundred dailies in 1909. Today, the number of daily newspapers is less than seventeen hundred. Although overall circulation is increasing for daily papers, it's a mixed picture. Morning circulation is increasing, and evening circulation is dropping. Furthermore, some major metropolitan papers are losing circulation to the growing number of suburban newspapers. There are also seventy-six hundred weekly newspapers, whose circulation is steadily expanding.

See if you can identify the three newspapers with the largest circulations today from the following list:

Wall Street Journal
New York Times
Detroit Free Press
Boston Globe
Los Angeles Times
Miami Herald
USA Today
Minneapolis Star Tribune

Your first choice should have been the *Wall Street Journal* followed by *USA Today* and the *New York Times*.

Falling circulation is not the only reason newspapers fail. The money that you put in a newspaper box or pay the carrier does not cover the cost of the labor and materials involved in producing the paper. Just like the magazine industry, the money to run newspapers comes mainly from advertising sales.

The *USA Today* Story

In the years since it first hit the newsstands on September 15, 1982, *USA Today* has become the second-largest newspaper in terms of circulation and the largest in terms of readership. More than six million people read *USA Today* five days a week. The newspaper employs more than twenty-one hundred people at thirty-six print sites. This paper is the first and only national, daily, general-interest newspaper in the United States.

Climbing to the Top as a Newspaper Editor

The climb to the top in the newspaper publishing industry is very similar to the book and magazine industries. Dennis Hetzel is a bookworm who has gone from writing for a local paper in high school to being the editor and publisher of the *York Daily Record* in York, Pennsylvania.

Starting Out in Newspaper Publishing. Dennis began his newspaper career in high school. Not being able to excel in sports, Dennis coupled his love of sports with his writing ability and free-lanced as a sports reporter for the local weekly. He majored in political science and minored in journalism in college and had plans to become a high school teacher—he even did his student teaching. However, an opportunity to become the sports editor for two weekly papers changed his career path. He believes that his high school sports writing experience got him this job. Working in sports, according to Dennis, requires a tremendous amount of reading each day just to keep track of what is happening.

After a year, Dennis went to another paper in Galesburg, Illinois, as a reporter. On this paper, one of his beats was the courts, which required the ability to read fast and to read for understanding. Dennis had to review lengthy, complicated documents and figure out what the important points were.

Climbing the Editorial Ladder. After taking a job as a reporter with another paper in Racine, Wisconsin, Dennis became special projects editor within a few years. He did a lot of research on this job; he read and edited others' work and researched special projects. Continuing his upward climb, Dennis became an associate editor. This job required him to supervise the copy desk and prepare the front page. He had to read stories coming in from outside news services and pick out the ones to use in the paper. Several hundred stories might be available, while there was room for only a few dozen.

Advancing to Managing Editor. In 1986, Dennis became managing editor of the *Capital Times* in Madison, Wisconsin. Half or more of his time was spent on managerial tasks. He read and wrote many memos, but he also read newspapers and articles in trade magazines such as *Editor & Publisher*. Besides reading his own newspaper, he read two or three other newspapers every morning plus an afternoon newspaper.

Becoming Editor and Publisher. In 1990, Dennis became the editor and publisher of the *York Daily Record*. As publisher, he is the chief operating officer and plays more of a role in community affairs. As editor, he is responsible for setting the overall policy and direction of the newspaper. Much of his reading today is concentrated on learning more about the information highway and where we are headed. Dennis still reads several newspapers a day; however, he finds that he is reading more online and sees a migration away from print. He believes that it is essential to read in order to succeed in the newspaper industry.

Copyediting for Newspapers

Copyediting requires on-the-job reading—not for just part of the day, but all day, every workday. Copyediting is the process of reviewing and editing the work of reporters so it is ready for layout. It involves finding and correcting spelling, grammar, and punctuation errors. Copyediting on a magazine or a book may involve fact checking, but copy is generally considered correct on newspapers. There just isn't time on a newspaper for checking facts beyond looking for obvious errors or inconsistencies.

Bookworms must realize that copyeditors do not sit in soft easy chairs leisurely editing. At most newspapers, they sit in front of computers staring at stories on monitors for hours. The pace is quite fast, as they hurry to get copy ready to be printed. Perhaps one of the best ways to determine if copyediting is for you is to read the requirements for a copyediting job on a large metropolitan newspaper with a circulation of several hundred thousand.

A Copyeditor's Job

Jim Lindgren is features copy desk chief in charge of eleven copy-editors at a major newspaper in the Midwest. At the start of the day, thirty or forty stories may be stored in the newspaper's computer system waiting to be edited. Reporters have written the stories and given them to their editors, who may have made some changes. Then the page designers place instructions on the stories detailing what kind of headlines are to be used and what the size of the story should be (column length). These stories are then assigned to rim editors by the slot editor, who parcels out assignments and makes sure that the copyeditors are working on what is needed. At most newspapers, all this is done by computer.

Jim pulls a story up on his computer monitor, and the copyediting process begins. According to journalism textbooks, stories should be read through completely first. With the time restraints of newspaper deadlines, this doesn't happen all the time. As Jim reads through the copy, he edits. For an experienced copyeditor like Jim, the errors usually jump out. He knows what words are always misspelled and even what mistakes individual reporters make. At times, he must do considerable rewriting to meet space specifications, which are so tight that he may substitute the word *try* for *attempt*. At the press of a button on his computer, Jim can tell whether the story is the correct length or not. When a story is the correct size, he writes a headline that tells the story and meets the space allotted for it. The story is then sent to the slot editor, who reads through it and approves the editing and headline.

Once all the stories on a page are completed, a proof is made and it is read to check for mistakes. When any mistakes have been corrected, the page is ready to appear in the paper.

When the first copies of the paper come out, Jim and the other copyeditors read through it and note any needed corrections on the paper. New stories in subsequent editions are also checked for errors.

Personal Qualifications of Copyeditors. You must have a love affair with words. You should enjoy playing with words. Most copyeditors are confirmed punsters. They also work crosswords, as Jim does, to learn smaller words for larger words. Above all, you need to be a bookworm who enjoys reading a wide variety of material both on and off the job. Jim met this qualification as a child—he always had his nose in adventure books.

Copyeditors typically have bachelor's degrees in English or journalism. Jim's is in journalism. At college, he worked on the student newspaper, which gave him experience in reporting, editing, and design and helped him discover that he enjoyed editing most of all. He advises future copyeditors to get a foot in the door by being willing to take any job that will allow them to work for a paper. He began his career as editor of a small-town weekly paper and then began copyediting at a small daily paper before moving to his present newspaper to begin the climb up the copyediting ladder.

The Newspaper Pay Scale

Whether your first job is working for a book publisher, a magazine publisher, or a newspaper, you will not be earning a high starting salary. Although some reporters work on union newspapers that negotiate their salaries with the Newspaper Guild, most don't. In 2000, the range of salaries for reporters stretched from a low of $16,500 per year to $69,300 for top reporters on major newspapers. The average annual salary for all reporters was nearly $27,000. Copyeditors usually receive comparable salaries to reporters.

Getting a Foot in the Door

You are most likely to get your first job in the newspaper industry because a reporter or copyeditor has left the industry, been promoted, or moved to a larger newspaper. Competition for jobs on major newspapers is fierce. Small-town and suburban papers offer better opportunities for finding that all-important first job. No matter where you get your first job, you are likely to be working for a newspaper chain because chains own more than 75 percent of all newspapers.

To get just about any entry-level job on a newspaper, you must have excellent word-processing skills. Computer graphics and desktop publishing skills may also be useful. Most employers will expect you to have a bachelor's degree in journalism, but some hire graduates with other majors. Experience is very important in getting a job. It is just about essential to be able to list an internship, part-time job, or summer job in the industry to secure your first newspaper job. It even helps to have worked on your high school or college newspaper.

Your Future in the Newspaper Industry

While newspapers are forecast to grow in the near future, greater emphasis will be placed on delivering to readers the specific information they want. New opportunities exist to become involved in publishing online newspapers. Many newspapers now have websites with some of the day's news. And the larger newspapers have very complete online news sites.

For bookworms, newspapers are an appealing career choice. Of course, not every employee reads for eight hours a day, but most do some reading. Furthermore, positions like copyeditor and wire editor offer almost eight hours a day of reading. The newspaper industry has more than four hundred thousand employees, which is nearly four times the number of people employed in the magazine industry. Perhaps you will be one of these employees in the future.

Two Satisfying Careers for Bookworms

What do people working on magazines and newspapers have in common? They usually love the work they do. They thrive on the excitement of deadlines, whether they are the deadlines for different editions of a newspaper or the weekly, monthly, or quarterly deadlines of magazines. They universally complain about low pay. They garner satisfaction from providing information so that people can know what is going on around them. Most of all, they savor working with words in some way. For, undeniably, jobs on both magazines and newspapers offer considerable opportunity to read.

For Further Reading

Because so many opportunities exist for employment in magazine and newspaper publishing, it is a good idea to look at directories that list the large number of companies in this field. All kinds of interesting job possibilities exist. You might find it possible to combine your interest in birds or clothing with working on a consumer specialty magazine. Perhaps your addiction to reading about current events would be satisfied through working on a newspaper. Information in the following books should be helpful.

Directories

Bacon's Magazine Directory. Chicago: Bacon's Information, annual.

Bacon's Newspaper Directory. Chicago: Bacon's Information, annual.

The Directory of Small Press & Magazine Editors & Publishers. Paradise, CA: Dustbooks, biannual.

The Standard Periodical Directory. New York: Oxbridge Communications, annual.

Books

Camenson, Blythe. *Careers in Publishing.* Chicago: VGM Career Books, 2000.

Johnson, Sammye, and Patricia Prijatel. *The Magazine from Cover to Cover: Inside a Dynamic Industry.* New York: McGraw-Hill, 2000.

Mogel, Leonard. *The Magazine: Everything You Need to Know to Make It in the Magazine Business.* Sewickley, PA: GATF Press, 2001.

Monti, Ralph. *Career Opportunities in Magazine Publishing: The Ultimate Guide to Succeeding in the Business.* Chicago: Independent Publishers Group, 1998.

Rocha, Toni L. *Careers in Magazine Publishing.* New York: The Rosen Publishing Group, 2000.

Wilson, Wayne. *Careers in Publishing and Communication.* Bear, DE: Mitchell Lane Publishers, 2001.

CHAPTER FIVE

Careers in Glamour Industries

Reading in the Limelight

How would you like to do a lot of reading while working closely with a radio, television, or movie personality—or even being in the limelight yourself? Someone has to read and analyze all the scripts submitted to television and movie companies. Every news and talk show on radio and television has people behind the scene reading about what is going on in the world that day. Public relations firms need readers to find out what others are saying about their clients in newspapers and magazines. Throughout all these glamour industries, there are many jobs at all levels that are perfect for bookworms.

The lure of working in some way in movies, television, radio, or public relations is so great that college graduates are fiercely competing for entry-level positions. Unfortunately, first jobs in these industries generally require long and hard hours and offer low pay. Preparation for one of these jobs is, however, up a bookworm's alley. You simply have to read as much as you can to get an idea of the basics of how radio and television shows are produced, movies are made, and public relations campaigns are handled.

Radio—the Vocal Medium

Many people don't realize that before television became so popular, families sat around their radios every evening. They listened to "Great Gildersleeve," "The Jack Benny Program," and "Inner

Sanctum Mysteries" for entertainment. They found out about what was happening in the world by listening to Lowell Thomas, Edward R. Murrow, and other famous news commentators. Some danced to the music of the big bands or Top 40 tunes. But this golden age of radio ended when television took over.

Radio did not roll over and play dead. Instead, radio changed its format. All-talk, all-news, and all-music stations emerged, as well as stations with formats designed to attract particular audiences. Soon radio had captured more listeners than ever before. In fact, homes today have a far greater number of radios than television sets. Perhaps part of this can be traced to the convenience of radio. You can drive a car and listen to the radio. You can jog down the street listening to a radio. You can listen to radios on buses, trains, and ferris wheels. The current popularity of radio means more jobs for people wanting to work in this medium. Many of these jobs are designed for people who love to talk and read.

Radio Deejays Read

Jeff Pigeon is a radio deejay on an adult contemporary program at WIBC in Indianapolis. Jeff is an early-morning bookworm—not a twenty-four-hour-a-day bookworm. Arriving at the station every morning at 4:15 for his 5:00 A.M. show, he begins reading immediately. He reads the local morning paper plus two other newspapers so he will know what has been happening locally and around the world when he goes on the air. His producer is also busily reading, giving Jeff highlighted articles to take to the studio.

While Jeff enjoys reading, he is definitely not a speed reader. Because he likes to take his time with the printed word and slowly absorb what he is reading, he does a lot of his reading at home. He always reads the evening paper along with a whole list of popular magazines and even the tabloids. Jeff is also kept busy trying to keep up with all the new books that publishers send to him. He has to resort to skimming many of these books.

Jeff is constantly preparing for his show. Everything that happens to him during the day as well as anything he reads could be a good topic of conversation on one of his shows. He feels that those who want to succeed in the radio industry will read as much material as they can get their hands on.

Talk-Show Hosts Read

You have probably listened to talk shows and may even have called in to offer your opinion on some topic. Many radio stations have an all-talk format, with hosting jobs that are perfect for bookworms. In order to do a talk show, it is absolutely essential to keep up-to-date with what is happening in the world. Barbara Simpson, the host of her own talk program on KSFO in San Francisco, loves this aspect of her job and believes it is why she can talk about anything and ad-lib with ease. Once the calls start coming, Barbara never knows what her audience will talk about. It could be one of the topics from her opening chat or a casual remark from a listener that captures everyone's interest. Barbara spends at least thirty hours a week reading in preparation for her program.

Each month Barbara will read more than fifty-five publications, from *People* to *National Review* to the *CDC Morbidity and Mortality Weekly Report*. Besides perusing local, regional, national, and international newspapers daily, she reads varied news wire and Internet resources. Barbara gets ideas for her program everywhere. A book review on espionage or a newspaper article on prenatal surgery may lead her to guests and show topics.

If you are drawn to a career in radio, Barbara advises finding an internship so you can evaluate whether this choice is really right for you. She also recommends getting a degree in liberal arts with an academic emphasis because it gives you the broad knowledge needed to measure today's events in light of history. You also need to love to talk.

Barbara's career extends beyond the boundaries of being a talk show host. She writes a column for worldnetdaily.com and does media and political consulting through her company, Blue Shadow Productions.

Radio-Show Producers Read

Susan Schustak is producer of the "Ronn Owens Show," which airs five mornings a week on KGO in San Francisco. This is a very popular news talk show that has people call in. Ronn, the host, interacts with the callers and also interviews guests. He is an avid reader, and so is Susan. Because Ronn's show airs in the morning, Susan regularly gets up at 5:30 A.M. so she can go through fifteen newspapers. With a solid knowledge of what has been going on in the world, she is ready to give Ronn her input on the list of topics for the show.

Part of Susan's job involves reading newspapers, news and pop-culture magazines, and websites to look for good guests, as well as moral issues for Ronn's personal opinion segment at the start of the show. During the show, she screens calls, looking for people with passion and divergent views to bring balance to the show. After the show, she discusses the next day's program with Ronn. Because Susan is an information junkie who loves to learn, she truly enjoys having a job that requires so much reading.

Movies—a Glamorous Environment for Readers

The movie industry is a rather small one, with fewer than a quarter-million people working in it. If your dream is to work in this industry, you should pack your bags and head for Southern California because it's still the center of moviemaking. Most of the movie jobs that are ideal for bookworms center on handling scripts. Some jobs put you in touch with the stars—from handling their fan mail to reading scripts for them. Some jobs also exist in doing research to determine that everything shown in a film is as authentic as possible. Whatever your job in this industry, the possibility of meeting famous stars and directors is always there.

The movie industry is a close-knit one. Getting a job seems to be tied to knowing someone who has a job or knows about a job.

The secret in finding the job you want often lies in taking an entry-level job that lets you make contacts in the industry and also acquaints you with the different types of jobs available. Reading also helps. By reading *Variety* and *Hollywood Reporter,* two dailies about the movie business, you can find out what is happening in every phase of the industry, from new film stars to movies currently in production.

A Possible Starting Point

There is a rumor that Woody Allen started as a script typist. Whether this is true or not, the job is one that gives you a look at a lot of scripts. Being a script typist is excellent preparation for becoming a story analyst or a screenwriter. After you have handled hundreds of scripts, you will learn what is good and thoroughly understand the format in which scripts are written.

According to Valerie Koutnik, who was a script typist in Hollywood and is now a screenwriter, the job involves taking a script and putting it into the correct format. There are many complex rules for the layout of dialogue and descriptive passages, with different styles for film and television.

The two basic requirements for getting a job as a script typist are: (1) you must be an excellent typist; (2) you must be a person who will safeguard the confidentiality of the scripts you type. Just think of how important script confidentiality is for the final television show of a season.

Valerie believes that a significant advantage of script-typing work is that it is one of the easier ways to get inside the film industry. Script typists can find work with independent production companies, studios, artists' agencies, freelance writers, and professional script-typing companies. You can find script-typing companies listed in the Los Angeles yellow pages.

Although the pay is hourly and the work can sometimes be tedious, Valerie feels it is invaluable experience in seeing how scripts are put together.

Working as a Story Analyst

Working as a story analyst involves reading movie scripts, books, and plays to find one that has the potential to be made as a movie that will earn money. The whole industry is searching for these movies, so there are jobs at agencies, studios, production companies, and with individual stars. To work at most studios, you have to belong to a union. There are many places where you can read without belonging to a union, as well as many opportunities to be a freelancer. A freelancer can earn from $25 at the low end of the scale to $50 at the high end for reading each script. The pay range is from $60 to $200 for books and longer-than-usual scripts.

The Job Description. Story analysts read movie scripts, books, and plays and write coverages. Each studio, production company, or agency will use a different form for coverages, which involve the following three things:

1. A synopsis is written that retells the story as clearly as possible. The length and detail of the synopsis vary with the story analyst's employer.
2. The story analyst's opinion is given, explaining whether or not the story has commercial value, is castable, and is similar to other movies or well-known books.
3. A rating scale is usually filled in that rates such things as production value, structure, characterization, and dialogue on a scale from poor to excellent.

Job Qualifications. No degree is required for the job of story analyst. However, the analyst should have developed a literary sense from a lot of reading and a visual sense from having seen a lot of movies. Story analysts also need to know how to write.

One Bookworm's Job as a Story Analyst

With a degree in film, radio, and television in hand, Randy Kornfield entered the job market with the desire to become a screenwriter. A friend got him a part-time job duplicating scripts at a studio. Then he was promoted to the mailroom. During this time he was meeting people and deciding where he wanted to work, as well as trying to write screenplays. A move to another studio brought Randy a job as a secretary and assistant in personnel. At this job, he met a story editor who let him read some scripts and write coverages. This gave him the chance to see what good and bad scripts were like, as well as what kinds of scripts were being bought. When this job folded, Randy became a freelance story analyst. Then he found a job at another studio as an assistant to an executive who was looking for scripts. At this job, which was primarily secretarial, he was able to read some scripts but didn't have to write coverages. After management changes at the studio, Randy was out of a job again. He next found a job as a story analyst at a nonunion studio. Then he was able to get a story analyst job at MGM, a union studio, because the story editor whom he met earlier was now working at this studio. This was followed by stints at 20th Century Fox and Sony Pictures. The advantage of working at a union studio is better pay plus benefits. Unfortunately, it is very difficult to get a job in a union studio.

During all this time, Randy has been busy writing and has met with considerable success as a beginning screenwriter. You may have seen his holiday movie *Jingle All the Way,* starring Arnold Schwarzenegger, or the feature *Eight-Legged Freaks.* He has also written several movies that were produced on television. Reading scripts has been helpful in his writing. Plus, he receives considerable satisfaction in discovering scripts that have been turned into successful movies, such as *Black Hawk Down* and *Life as a House.*

Story Analyst for a Movie Star

Would you like to talk to a movie star on the phone or perhaps have him or her come to your office several times a week? All of this was part of Sandy Erickson's job as a story analyst when she read scripts and books looking for the right properties for Matt Dillon.

This was a glamour job that let Sandy read 70 percent of the time. You can find jobs like hers in the offices of managers and agents of movie stars.

Reading Fan Mail

Movie stars get loads of letters from their fans. Almost all of this mail is handled by a fan club service provided by a star's manager, agent, or studio. Most of the letters are from people simply requesting pictures. The rest of the letters can usually be answered by form letters. Only a few letters require a personal reply.

Running a Production Company

This is a glamorous job that let Matt Levy read 50 percent of the time while running Kiefer Sutherland's production company at 20th Century Fox. Matt spent much of his day searching for the right property for Kiefer to act in, produce, or direct. This involved reading a lot of scripts and books as well as newspapers and magazines for ideas. Matt also met with writers and listened to pitches—all to find possibilities for Kiefer's consideration.

Many actors have someone who reads for them because they don't have the time to evaluate all the materials out there when they are working. There are literally hundreds of ways to get these jobs—from starting in the mail room and building relations with people in the industry to working with an actor on a movie as Matt did with Kiefer. When you land a job like this, you may find yourself employed by a very eccentric actor, or you may be as lucky as Matt was and find yourself working for someone very pleasant. In any case, there is a lot of competition for these jobs.

Television—Almost Everyone's Favorite Medium

In the United States, television sets are found in 98 percent of all homes, and these sets are on for an average of more than seven hours a day. From the crack of dawn until late at night, there are many households where the television set is rarely off. People can be totally entertained right in their own homes just by turning on their television sets. They can find whatever interests them, whether it is movies, quiz shows, soap operas, cartoons, educational programs, situation comedies, action-packed dramas, variety shows, news shows, or sports events. What is significant to the job seeker is that each show requires more people behind the scenes than the ones seen on the television screen. And many television jobs, both on camera and off, are good choices for bookworms who want jobs that require considerable reading.

Network Story Editor

DeNece Gilbert knew that she wanted to work for a large television network even before she graduated from college with a communications degree. So after graduation she headed west—straight for Hollywood. Not knowing anyone and without any experience, she couldn't get a job in television. She did get a job in the publishing division of Motown Records, which required her to place songs with the appropriate Motown artists.

After gaining experience at Motown, DeNece became a secretary at a major network. Several promotions later, she was the assistant to the director of comedy and drama. This job was a bookworm's delight. DeNece's job was to read scripts and treatments and to write a one-page synopsis of each work for the director. She worked on the weekly episodes of many popular shows.

Today, DeNece is working for a major network in New York City as a story editor covering books. It is her job to find books that would make good television movies or miniseries. She works with thirty large publishing houses in New York and thirty other smaller publishing houses throughout the country. Her only job is to look for good stories. DeNece does not do any writing or rewriting. The network hires writers or uses in-house writers for any changes or adaptations that are needed.

On the job, most of DeNece's reading time is spent going through publishing catalogs. She usually orders ten or eleven books from each catalog. DeNece also looks through the *Kirkus Review*, which lists upcoming books, and *Publishers Weekly*. She reads popular consumer magazines as well as newspapers to discover future trends. She usually takes manuscripts and books home to read so that she can read them without interruption.

DeNece can't read everything, so she has ten freelance readers who keep busy reading for her. They write a two-and-one-half-page summary of each book, plus a one-page personal comment sheet. If a freelancer suggests a second reading or praises the work, DeNece reads the material. It takes more than one year from the time material goes into development until it is seen on the air. DeNece looks for fresh work and often goes for first-time authors.

Glamour does enter into this ideal job for a bookworm. The casting office is right next to DeNece's office. There are trips to large book fairs and the Louisville Playwriter's Festival. At this festival, she is not only looking at the plays but is also on the lookout for good new writers.

According to DeNece, networks have many other jobs that bookworms would like. Script readers are needed for every division in a network. For the children's after-school specials, the readers even read children's books to find new program ideas. There are also jobs for research librarians.

Producers of Talk Shows

All those talk shows you see on television have producers. Some even have producers for each segment of the show. These producers are responsible for what happens on a show—a job usually requiring considerable reading.

A talk-show producer may read the books of authors who are going to be on the program and then frame questions for the talk-show host. Then there are all the books that land on the talk-show producer's desk; these must be looked at to see which authors should be selected to appear on the program. Research may also be done on each guest on the program to acquaint the host with the day's guest or guests. Furthermore, there is the task of keeping up with what is happening in the world so provocative guests and subjects can be chosen. A daily talk show consumes a lot of material, so the search for new ideas is never ending. Most of these ideas will evolve from the reading done by the show's producer or producers.

Jobs as producers and segment producers are not usually entry-level jobs, except at smaller television stations. To be a producer of a major network show requires previous experience. A producer might start at a station as an assistant, advance to associate producer, and then be a coordinating producer before becoming a producer.

A News-Show Producer

Producers of TV talk shows aren't the only ones who read. Producers of news shows also must read. Mike Weir produces the "KRON 4 News at 5" show for a major station in San Francisco. This is a late-afternoon half-hour show that is aired Monday through Friday. The show deals mainly with local and national news of the day. After the top news stories have aired, the stories are geared toward medicine, women, children, consumer issues, and other topics appropriate for the time slot's audience.

Producers like Mike read all day long. Before work, he has read three newspapers and several news magazines to put topics in perspective, and he keeps reading AP wire service material all day long to keep himself constantly updated on what is happening in the world. He must have this knowledge as he decides the editorial content of the news show in collaboration with the producers of other news shows. Mike is also busy determining the order in which stories will be presented on the show, the look of the show, the graphics that will be used, the use of live shots, and the myriad details that guarantee a smooth production.

Producing a news show is not just reading. Mike does loads of writing for the program. Writing for television is quite different from writing for other media. The language must be simple, and so must the sentences. On his show, the writing must be for the ear because many people at this time in the afternoon are viewing TV while doing other things.

Mike started working in television as the weekend producer of a news show in a small market. He was able to do this because he attended a college that had a broadcasting program that allowed him to get experience producing shows while he was still in school.

News Reporters Need to Read

If you write the scripts for news reports on television, then you will need to read for information. You simply can't do an in-depth treatment of a topic without having background information on it. To keep abreast of what is going on in the world for his job as a television news reporter for an NBC affiliate, David MacAnally reads daily papers, including the *New York Times,* plus news feature magazines.

News Anchor on a Midwest Station

Maybe some anchors are just performers. However, Tom Cochrun, former evening news anchor at an NBC station in Indianapolis, was not one of them. Tom is a true bookworm who, as a child, stayed up many evenings with a flashlight trying to finish sports adventure books that got him hooked on reading.

In his job as news anchor, Tom read for 60 to 80 percent of his workday. He read newspapers, research reports, background reports, and magazines. Tom felt that in order to write news copy that his viewers would understand, he had to have a strong grasp of the information. He says he could not get this understanding from just reading wire-service information. Tom Brokaw, Judy Woodruff, Paula Zahn, Peter Jennings, and Ted Koppel are other anchors who do a great deal of reading to prepare for their shows.

Public Relations

Companies, institutions, unions, activist groups, and all kinds of organizations want to win public approval. The people who do this job for them are in the public relations field, which is commonly called PR. Some organizations have their own public relations departments, while others use public relations firms. In either case, the task is to communicate with a specific audience. Airlines may want to stress how safe it is to fly after several crashes have shaken the public's confidence in air travel. A chemical company may want to reassure its workers on the safety of the workplace. A food company may want to communicate to its stockholders the reasons why the price of its stock is steadily falling.

People employed in public relations work have two main activities: research and communication. Most of the glamour lies in the communication side because PR people arrange for media publicity. It is the research side that allows bookworms to read. In order to handle an account, it is essential to be well versed in what a client does. This may mean not only reading about a company but also an entire industry. The majority of reading is probably done to find out what newspapers and magazines are writing about clients. It is also important to gather information that may affect a client. Today's public relations employees are voracious readers who must read everything in order to serve their clients effectively.

Travel Agents

The type of reading that travel agents do is frequently investigative. Cynthia Kroos, the managing director of a travel agency, finds it essential to learn about new tourist spots, resorts, and tours. She is constantly reading trade publications to do this. Obviously, a lot of reading also has to be done to keep up with all the packages that are offered by airlines and tour companies. According to Cynthia, travel agents have so much reading to do that it can almost bury them. Because so much of the workday is devoted to dealing with clients, considerable reading must be done at home. The glamorous bonus to all of this reading is the frequent trips that Cynthia takes to learn more about places her clients may wish to visit.

Reading Can Be Glamorous

While a glamour career may be appealing to many people, including bookworms, it is not easy to break into a glamorous field. Even college graduates are usually required to begin in low-level positions because experience is needed for the positions they seek. Few have that experience, so graduates are often forced to begin as secretaries, typists, or gofers to gain experience. There is always room for good people in glamour industries. However, getting the job of your dreams involves hard work as well as luck, perseverance, and good timing.

Glamour careers at all levels can be pressure filled and tension packed as people struggle to meet deadlines for such things as television shows, advertising promotions, and the production of movies. There is no guarantee of a nine-to-five job. Like all careers, considerable drudgery is involved. However, glamour careers do offer involvement in exciting industries such as radio, television, the movies, travel, and public relations, which makes these careers so sought after.

For Further Reading

The more you know about the glamour industries, the easier it will be for you to discover the job you want. A surprising number of jobs in this industry are filled by people who read for a substantial period of time each day. While most bookworms are working behind the scenes in these industries, a few are also in the public eye. The following books should give you a better idea of what careers are available in the glamour industries.

Bone, Jan, and Kathy Siebel. *Opportunities in Film Careers.* Chicago: VGM Career Books, 1998.

Elsenpeter, Robert C. *Get into Radio.* Seattle: Fender Publishing Company, 1998.

Mogel, Leonard. *Careers in Communications and Entertainment.* New York: Kaplan Publishing, 2000.

Mogel, Leonard. *Making It in Public Relations: An Insider's Guide to Career Opportunities.* Mahaw, NJ: Lawrence Erlbaum Associates, 2002.

Noronha, Shonan. *Careers in Communications.* Chicago: VGM Career Books, 1998.

Noronha, Shonan. *Opportunities in Television and Video Careers.* Chicago: VGM Career Books, 1998.

Rotman, Morris B.; Luisa Gerasimo; and Robert W. Galvin. *Opportunities in Public Relations Careers.* Chicago: VGM Career Books, 2001.

Rubin, Karen. *Inside Secrets to Finding a Career in Travel.* Concord, Ontario: Career Lifeskills Resources, 2001.

CHAPTER SIX

Careers in Education

Passing Knowledge on to the Next Generation

Today a reader, tomorrow a leader.
— W. Fusselman

ooks are an integral part of teaching. Successful teachers love books, read books, and understand them. However, being a bookworm is not enough to make someone a good teacher. Good teachers must also be able to pass the knowledge, skills, and information that they have acquired from books on to their students. It is appropriate that teaching is the largest profession in the world. If there were no teachers, people would have to learn so much on their own, and so much of the knowledge that has been accumulated from past generations would disappear.

Preparing to Teach

Teaching is not a new profession. Scholars like Aristotle, Plato, and Socrates were teachers. But it was not until the 1800s that teaching schools began to develop. Today, anyone planning to teach, whether in a kindergarten or at the college or university level, needs a college degree. Many elementary, middle school, junior high, and high school teachers also need to get master's degrees to advance in the profession and to increase earnings. Bookworms who want to teach at the college level will find it is very helpful to have doctorates. Prospective elementary, middle school, junior high, and senior high school teachers study similar courses during their first two years of college. These are basic liberal arts courses and include the study of history, language arts, mathematics, and science. During their college years, they also take teaching methods courses and do actual practice teaching in a classroom under the guidance of an experienced teacher. In addition, future high school teachers specialize in the particular subject areas in which they plan to teach.

Before most bookworms can start teaching, they need to meet state requirements for teacher certification. These requirements deal with the college courses that teachers must complete satisfactorily to become certified as elementary, middle school, junior high, and senior high school teachers in the public schools. Each state has different requirements. In some states, teachers at nursery schools, private schools, and junior colleges also have to be certified. However, teachers at four-year colleges and universities do not need state certification.

Generic Teaching Duties

All teachers, no matter what level they are teaching, have a number of duties that must be performed—from taking attendance to filling out report cards.

Getting Ready. Bookworms find classroom preparation enjoyable because it involves so much reading. Teachers read textbooks, teacher's manuals, course-related materials, professional journals, and curriculum guides to prepare for their daily stint in the classroom. However, preparation goes beyond reading to making sure everything is completely ready for each lesson. Materials have to be duplicated. Supplementary books and materials as well as supplies have to be obtained and laid out in readiness for each class.

Leading the Way. Teachers are the classroom leaders. Through a variety of teaching methods, they have to motivate their students to learn, show them how to learn, and instill intellectual curiosity in them. Books help teachers in this task, as do all kinds of audiovisual materials, such as CDs, tapes, filmstrips, videos, movies, and television programs, plus all the things that can be done with computers.

Checking Progress. All teachers need to make sure that their students have learned the material. Mastery is important, whether it is the alphabet, the multiplication tables, or French grammar. Teachers check their students' progress through analyzing written and oral work and quizzes and tests. Records need to be kept so that teachers know how each individual student is doing. This information must be placed on report cards and discussed at conferences with parents.

Being a Role Model. Students do notice how their teachers behave. Younger students, especially, often want to be just like their teachers. Teachers set a very powerful example for their students through their own sincerity, patience, kindness, understanding, honesty, and objectivity. Furthermore, teachers who truly love to read inspire their students to become lifelong readers, and a new generation of bookworms emerges.

Doing the Extra Tasks. Teachers have other obligations besides routine classroom tasks. They are also expected to take a share of duties, such as hall and playground duty and supervising the lunchroom and bus loading. They chaperone many after-school events, attend faculty meetings, and sponsor clubs. You should not consider teaching as a profession if you expect to be home by 3 P.M. each day.

A Closer Look at Teaching

Today, education is both America's largest business and profession. There are more than 3.8 million teachers in the United States, and more than $3 billion is spent on education every school day in this country. The good news for people interested in this profession is that the number of students attending school will increase, which raises the demand for teachers. The demand for secondary school teachers will be especially strong because student enrollment is growing fastest at this level. Also, more teachers are retiring, and there is a recent trend toward smaller class sizes, both of which further increase the need for teachers.

Teaching at the Lower Elementary Level

For bookworms, teaching children in the lower elementary grades can be very satisfying. These teachers have the opportunity to actually teach young children how to read and to help each child develop an appreciation for books. It is a chance for bookworms to instill their love of books in others.

According to Fran Hageboeck, a first-grade teacher for many years, half of her teaching day is devoted to some aspect of teaching reading. During that time, she reads out loud to the class for thirty minutes. Time is also spent having children read to her and listening to them read to each other. Away from the classroom, she spends time in the library searching for books to read to the children and for them to read. Of course, first-grade teachers teach subjects besides reading. They also spend time tying shoes, buttoning coats, putting on boots, and handing out tissues. But reading is the main focus of all the learning activities in first grade.

Teaching at the Upper Elementary or Middle School Level

If you were turned off by the need to tie shoes and button coats at the lower elementary level but still like children, you might find it more enjoyable to teach in one of the upper elementary grades or in middle school. In fourth, fifth, and sixth grades, students can handle all their own personal needs and have also mastered the basic reading skills. Teachers at these grade levels are helping students become independent learners. Besides classes in reading and mathematics, students are now beginning to learn in the content areas of history, science, health, and English. For bookworms, it is an opportunity to help children expand their horizons through a broad reading program.

The trend today is to teach thematic units in which students study a topic such as California and learn about its history, geography, and geology throughout the day as they study social studies, language arts, science, and mathematics. Searching for materials to use in this approach has Karen McCall, a fourth-grade teacher, reading avidly. Then, to keep up with what is happening in her profession, she reads newsletters and professional journals. Finally, she reads local papers and periodicals to keep abreast of community happenings. For Karen, reading plays an important role in the quality of instruction she brings to the classroom.

Teaching at the Junior High Level

Sue Engledow, a true bookworm, made a career change from being a bank manager to being a junior high school science teacher. Sue decided that she wanted to spend more time with books than with numbers. She went back to college and took the required education courses. Due to the influence of an elementary science teacher, Sue decided to become a science teacher. Sue has been teaching science to seventh graders in a suburban junior high school for more than ten years.

Sue finds that science teachers do considerable reading. She usually has one concentrated preparation period each week. During this time, she reads for three to four hours. Besides reading the teacher's manual, she reads the students' book, then she takes notes and makes outlines for herself and her students. Arriving an hour early every morning gives Sue the time to read over all her notes and outlines for the day, along with reading and preparing for the laboratory work her students will be doing.

Sue's reading time is not just devoted to preparation for her classes. She prepares all her own tests, so she has to spend more hours rereading all the material to develop these tests. If she gives an essay test, she has to spend additional hours reading the students' papers. Sue reads for another two to three hours every evening so that she is able to enhance what her students are reading in their textbooks.

Teaching at the High School Level

Giving students objectives before each reading assignment is Felice Knarr's way of developing critical readers in her twelfth-grade English literature classes. Felice has been teaching English at a private high school for several years.

In August, before school starts, Felice charts out her course of study for the entire school year. She reads every book that the students will be reading so that she knows how long each reading assignment should take.

This is not the only time Felice reads the material that will be assigned to her students. Before each reading assignment is made, she rereads the material to develop the objectives for her lesson plans. Beyond all the reading that Felice does in her preparation, she also spends six to eight hours a week grading the essays and compositions of her one hundred students. This does not include the reading that she must do in grading vocabulary, spelling, and short writing assignments.

Felice is a true bookworm who seems to always be reading. She spends several hours each day reading academic journals. It is common for her to spend eight to twelve hours on weekends keeping up with her academic reading because she is taking courses to complete her master's degree in English. For relaxation, Felice likes to read magazines.

Teaching at the College Level

The usual entry teaching position at the college level is as an assistant professor. Then the battle commences to get tenure, which is permanent faculty status. During the trial years before tenure is granted, which ranges from seven to ten years, assistant professors struggle to make names for themselves. The usual method at universities is by publishing papers for journals and books. This is the reason for the expression "publish or perish."

During this probationary period, reading fills every spare minute of an assistant professor's time, as research is done to produce the needed publications. The reading at this stage must necessarily be quite narrow within the teaching field. After the desired tenure is granted, reading can become much broader so that a fuller understanding of a field of study is achieved.

Assistant professors eventually become associate and then full professors, and some even become department chairpersons. Reading is an absolute necessity throughout an academic career. Teachers at the college level must keep up with what is happening in their individual fields and must read to develop new courses.

All Kinds of Teachers

There are many other teachers besides classroom teachers. Today, most elementary and middle schools have reading, speech, music, and physical education teachers on their teaching staffs. These teachers have specialized in a particular subject area, just as teachers in junior and senior high schools do. There are also teachers who work in gifted and talented programs and in special education. Some teachers become counselors, curriculum directors, and principals.

Other Positions in Education

Bookworms who are interested in education but don't want to work in the classroom can find satisfying jobs besides teaching that involve reading.

College Admissions Counselor

According to Steve Bushouse, former dean of admissions at Butler University in Indianapolis, you need strong basic reading skills to work as an admissions counselor at a college. However, he points out that you need to have other skills, too, in order to be successful at this job. Counselors in the admissions office also need to be very people oriented. Not only do admissions counselors interview students, they also give speeches at schools and work in booths at college fairs.

College admissions counselors read and evaluate high school records. Then, as part of a committee, they decide which students will be admitted to the college. In this job, entire days—often far into the night—are spent reading. Furthermore, this is not a five-day-a-week job, especially when applications are being read.

Curriculum Director

Within most large school districts, there are jobs for curriculum directors. Some may be in charge of an area such as elementary or high school curriculums, while others direct the curriculum of a single subject area, such as reading, mathematics, or science. In any case, this is one job that involves a great deal of reading as new textbooks are selected and new curriculums are developed.

State Education Administrator

The Department of Education in each state has advisory positions that would appeal to bookworms. One position that involves reading is working as a reading consultant. These consultants need to read widely so that they can advise teachers on the wide variety of materials that can be used in the classroom. Jobs in curriculum planning should also interest bookworms.

Education Association Professional

In the United States, there are many professional organizations for teachers. The National Education Association (NEA) has the largest membership. The American Federation of Teachers (AFT) is a teaching union that works to improve teaching conditions. There are also professional associations, such as the National Association of Secondary School Principals. All of the education organizations and associations offer jobs for bookworms in different capacities, ranging from researching to copyediting.

Travel Opportunities for Teachers

If you are a bookworm who likes to travel, there are many teaching jobs in all parts of the world. The pay is not always as good as it is in the United States, but the opportunities for travel and adventure are often an added pull for bookworms looking for excitement. If you are interested in working abroad as a teacher, you may want to visit the websites or write to some of the organizations listed here.

Fulbright Teacher and Administrator Exchange
Graduate School
U.S. Department of Agriculture
600 Maryland Avenue SW, Suite 320
Washington, DC 20024
www.grad.usa.gov/info_for/fulbright.cfm

Office of Overseas Schools
U.S. Department of State
Room H328, SA-1
Washington, DC 20522
www.state.gov/m/a/os

Peace Corps
Paul D. Coverdell Peace Corps Headquarters
1111 Twentieth Street NW
Washington, DC 20526
www.peacecorps.gov

International Schools Services
15 Roszel Road
P.O. Box 5910
Princeton, NJ 08543
www.iss.edu

U.S. Department of Defense
Education Activity
4040 North Fairfax Drive
Arlington, VA 22201
www.odedodea.edu

Teacher Salaries

Teachers' salaries are constantly increasing, although they vary greatly among states. Can you guess which state has the highest salary for teachers? Is it California, New York, Alaska, New Jersey, Hawaii, or Connecticut? If you picked Connecticut, you are correct; New Jersey is a close second. If you are interested in knowing what the starting salaries for schools in your area are, you can get this information from your state Department of Education or your local school district. The average starting salaries for all teachers range from the low twenties to the mid thirties.

Teachers' salaries usually increase each year based on merit, years of experience, and educational degrees. Secondary-school teachers in some states receive higher pay than elementary teachers. The average salary for college professors is more than $55,000 a year for full-time faculty members on nine-month contracts.

For Further Reading

Teaching is a bookworm's career today more than ever. The responsibilities and workloads of teachers have increased along with the volume of reading that must be done in order to keep pace with the rapid accumulation of knowledge. The following books provide a good look at what the teaching profession is like.

Eberts, Marjorie, and Mary McGowan. *Opportunities in Education Careers.* Chicago: VGM Career Books, 2000.

Echaore-McDavid, Susan. *Career Opportunities in Education.* New York: Checkmark Books, 2000.

Feirsen, Robert, and Seth Wietzman. *How to Get the Teaching Job You Want: The Complete Guide for College Graduates, Returning Teachers and Career Changers.* Sterling, VA: Stylus Publishing, 2001.

Fine, Janet. *Opportunities in Teaching Careers.* Chicago: VGM Career Books, 2000.

Moffatt, Courtney W., and Thomas Moffatt. *How to Get a Teaching Job.* Boston: Allyn & Bacon, 1999.

CHAPTER SEVEN

Careers in Research

Searching for Information

I f you are curious and would like to know more about any subject in the world, a career in research may be right for you. Whether you are interested in history, the environment, politics, religion, education, or a variety of other topics, this is one career that involves a great deal of reading. As the amount of information is constantly increasing, the need for more people in this relatively small job area continues to grow. In addition to reading books, periodicals, and other documents, many of today's researchers do a considerable amount of work on the Internet.

Research jobs involve searching for information so that papers, books, and reports can be written by university and research center scholars and historians. They also involve reading material so that it can be sorted into some kind of order. Much research is also done for local, state, and federal governments; museums; businesses; and special-interest groups.

More than any other country in the world, the United States has recognized the importance of research in both the public and private sectors, as indicated by the mind-boggling number of research organizations. There are thousands of university and profit and nonprofit research organizations. Many of these organizations, however, have small staffs.

Research Jobs at Universities

Universities are true research centers. A large university has numerous research projects going on all the time. Jobs become available whenever a new project is started. Many university projects are headed by resident faculty members; others are led by accomplished scholars from other universities who have come to the university to work on a research project. To head a project, you must have outstanding credentials. A doctorate degree is the basic requirement. Then you have to demonstrate that you are an expert in your field.

Fortunately for those who want to be researchers at a university, research projects need to have more staff people than the one person heading the project. In some cases, the lead researcher may only work at it part-time, leaving a lot of work for staff researchers. Although people seeking research staff positions don't need the same professional status as the project heads, they do need top-notch qualifications to land these desirable jobs. The competition for jobs as entry-level research assistants can be so intense at prestigious universities that you could be competing against fifty or more applicants.

The Research Assistant Job

There are different levels of research assistants. To climb each rung on the ladder, or to start beyond an entry-level position, you need more than a bachelor's degree, plus experience. You also have to demonstrate that you can evaluate and analyze what you read. As you move to higher levels, your responsibilities increase. You may become responsible for a phase of a project or an entire project.

You can find out about entry-level jobs in research through university employment offices, bulletins, and websites. These jobs do not require as much reading as bookworms would probably like. Usually, you can expect to spend about half of your time extracting information—that's the reading portion of the job—and the other half doing clerical work. In fact, having some clerical experience and knowing how to use a computer are prerequisites for getting entry-level jobs.

As a research assistant, you usually only work on one project at a time. This does give you the opportunity to become an expert on a subject through your reading. Some projects have a time limit, while others go on as more funding becomes available. After one project is finished, researchers typically go on to work on another project.

....

Research Jobs at Think Tanks

If you are constantly reading newspapers and news magazines to keep up with what is going on in the world and would like to do this for a living, then a job at a think tank could be ideal for you. Think tanks are a twentieth-century phenomenon made up of groups of researchers who seek and analyze information for governmental units, special-interest groups, businesses, and the public. This information is primarily used by government policy makers and bureaucrats to make decisions on policies. A researcher at a think tank could have a role in influencing legislation on the proper amount of financial aid for a Southeast Asian country or environmental controls on mining operations.

When you hear the words *think tank*, you may conjure up visions of intellectuals concentrating on heady problems. It is decidedly true that considerable thinking goes on at think tanks, but much of that thinking is based upon reading and research.

When the first think tanks emerged in the early decades of this century, research resulted in books and papers that influenced public decisions. Many of today's think tanks are more activist. While still producing books and papers, think tanks also actively lobby legislators and court the press to influence the government. So, besides researching and writing, the think tank employee's job description has to be rewritten to include public relations work.

The first generation of think tanks was slightly to the left or right of center in political thinking. However, research tended to show both viewpoints. During the volatile 1960s, specialized think tanks that considered only one issue began to evolve. Many of today's think tanks have strong conservative or liberal roots; however, some of the newer think tanks are taking more objective views. Nevertheless, people thinking of applying for a job at a think tank should probably consider their own political biases when deciding where to look for a job. Note the political leanings of the following prominent think tanks:

CONSERVATIVE
American Enterprise Institute for Public Policy Research
Cato Institute
Heritage Foundation
Hoover Institution
Hudson Institute

LIBERAL
Center for Defense Information
Center for National Policy
Institute for Policy Studies
Social Accountability International
World Policy Institute

If you wanted to work in North Dakota or Florida, you would have had trouble until recently finding a job with a think tank. There are now a few state-based think tanks concerned with state, not national, issues. Traditionally, most think tanks are located close to Washington, D.C., or New York City, although there are exceptions. One of the earliest conservative think tanks, the Hoover Institution, which was founded in 1919, is located in California. The Hudson Institute really overturned the East Coast emphasis by moving from a location forty-five miles from New York City to Indianapolis, Indiana, in 1984.

Working at a Think Tank
You may bump into people like Gerald Ford, Henry Kissinger, Mikhail Gorbachev, or Zbigniew Brzezinski if you work at a think tank. Many of the high-level jobs are held by people who have

been in the public limelight. Of course, most of the people working at think tanks don't have names that you see every day in the newspaper. But many are quite well-known scholars in their fields of expertise or show promise of being future academic superstars. At the older think tanks, you are more likely to work with well-known scholars and people who have made their names in government. Lawrence Summers, who was the secretary of the treasury under Clinton, is now at the Brookings Institution, while former United Nations Ambassador Jeane Kirkpatrick is at the American Enterprise Institute for Public Policy Research. The stars at the newer think tanks tend to be political activists instead of former government officials.

First-Level Researcher

If your vision of the perfect job is one where your desk is inundated with reading materials, an entry-level job at a think tank may be the right one for you. To get this type of job, impressive credentials are needed. For most jobs, some type of graduate degree—usually a master's degree—is essential. You also should have some experience in doing research, even if it is only writing your own research papers. When seeking a job, it can be helpful to know someone involved in a project at a think tank in order to discover what jobs are available; however, sending out resumes is also a good way to get a job.

If you have a job as a first-level researcher, you can work on researching just one topic for a think tank scholar or on a number of topics for different people. When a project starts, you will read to get a basic understanding of an issue. Then you may be asked to develop a bibliography for the head of the project. At times, you will summarize what you read. You may even be given a particular issue on which to focus. You will have considerable autonomy in deciding how your job will be performed. Ultimately, scholars at the think tank write papers or books on the topics that have been researched.

To advance up the ladder from a first-level researcher, a doctorate is usually required. To get a feel for what a job is like at a think tank, you should consider taking an internship at one of these institutions.

························

Archivists

Not too many people are acquainted with what archives are or what archivists do. First of all, archives are records of individuals, groups, institutions, and governments at all levels that are preserved because they have information of lasting value. Such historic documents as the Declaration of Independence, the U.S. Constitution, and the Bill of Rights are preserved in the National Archives Building in Washington, D.C. All of the valuable documents from each president's term of office are preserved in presidential libraries, which are archives. You can also find the records that must be kept by law for local and state governments in archives. Archival records are not just government documents. Businesses have archives; so do universities, hospitals, labor unions, and even small historical societies.

Records may be saved on any medium, including paper, film, videotape, audiotape, or electronic data. They also may be copied onto some other format to protect the original and make them more accessible to researchers who use the records.

The Job of an Archivist

The primary job of an archivist is to establish control over records. This involves organizing records so that they can easily be accessed. A collection must have a title, and all of the contents must be organized in a logical sequence and described so they can be used. The job also requires a judgment of what records have historical value; for example, the federal government only saves 3 percent of its records. Much of the work of the archivist, therefore, is going through documents to decide which should be kept permanently. All of these tasks require reading. Not only must the documents be read, the archivist needs to have an understanding of the historical period in which they were created to understand their value.

Another job of the archivist is overseeing the preservation of documents. Because original newsprint will not last, the archivist must supervise the reproduction of newspaper clippings onto acid-free paper. Archivists must also determine whether to restore or conserve an original document by microfilming or some other technique or to both restore and reproduce the original. The preservation is done by scientific and technical specialists.

The archivist's job also includes gathering information that is requested. Archivists are becoming more involved, too, in the publication and exhibition of materials. In addition, some archivists have the task of soliciting funds to preserve or establish a collection. And, of course, archivists who are in charge of collections have administrative responsibilities involved in supervising a staff.

What you earn as an archivist varies with where you work and live. Generally, the larger or better-funded institutions offer larger salaries. Beginning salaries typically range from the high twenties to the low thirties.

Requirements for Becoming an Archivist

After a person decides to be an archivist, it is usually a lifetime career. At first, archivists may move from one archive to another, but most eventually stay in one place. And that place may well be a governmental unit because the majority of archivists have civil service standing. Those who work at universities may also be faculty members.

The one personal characteristic that archivists have in common, no matter where they work, is an interest in preserving the past. There is also a need for organizational ability, good judgment, an interest in research, and self-reliance.

While there may be some entry-level jobs that require only a bachelor's degree, a master's degree is much more common. Undergraduate majors can vary, but master's degrees are usually in either history or library science. Increasingly, job candidates have master's degrees in both areas, with course work in the theory and practice of archives. Currently, there are very few college programs offering bachelor's or master's degrees in archival science. For senior staff positions, especially at universities, a doctorate may be required.

The archival profession is a growing one. One way to learn more about this profession is by contacting:

Society of American Archivists (SAA)
527 Wells Street, Fifth Floor
Chicago, IL 60607
www.archivists.org

....

Curators

Like archivists, curators are concerned with keeping records of the past. The difference is that archivists are primarily concerned with written materials, and curators are primarily concerned with objects and specimens. You will find curators at museums, zoos, aquariums, botanic gardens, and historic sites. Curators who work for the federal government are found at the Smithsonian Institution, military museums, and in archeological and other museums run by the Department of the Interior.

The Curator's Job

A curator's job varies depending on the size of the place where the curator works. In a small institution, the curator must not only acquire, identify, catalog, and store objects but also restore objects, arrange for exhibitions, and conduct educational programs. This job description can be further expanded to include doing all the research and the hammering and nailing when it comes to setting up an exhibition. At a large institution, a curator might specialize in a particular area—such as toys, anthropology, science, or technology—or be assigned a function—such as cataloging, acquisitions, or restoration of the collection.

Whether a curator has a specific responsibility or is responsible for everything at an institution, considerable reading is essential in this job. When an institution acquires new objects or specimens, curators must read to identify them accurately. When a new exhibit is being set up, the curator researches to see what belongs in the exhibit and that everything is properly displayed. Curators must also read to find out about the newest and best ways to preserve and display objects and specimens. There is also reading to answer questions posed by the public. And, of course, considerable reading of professional journals is essential to keep up with what is happening in the profession.

Requirements for Becoming a Curator

While some curators have earned bachelor's or master's degrees in museum studies (museology), many institutions are looking for curators with degrees in specific areas such as art, anthropology, biology, or history.

The minimum requirements for obtaining a curator's job are a bachelor's degree and experience. Most museums, however, want curators to have a master's degree in a specific field plus experience. Curators working in smaller institutions may also need some business courses to handle administrative responsibilities.

There are fewer than twenty-five thousand jobs for archivists and curators, but because of the current interest in art, history, technology, and culture, the number of curators is growing. However, there will never be a great number of openings for jobs as curators.

Furthermore, the job is appealing to many qualified applicants, so there is considerable competition. Those who have had experience as interns or volunteers often have the best chance to get these coveted jobs. Curators' salaries are similar to those of archivists, from the high twenties to the low thirties.

....

Historians

Why did Winston Churchill lose his post as prime minister after successfully leading Britain through World War II? How successful was the first Five-Year Plan in China in terms of stimulating agricultural production? Historians formulate questions like these to direct their studies of the past. They are imaginative researchers who read all kinds of documents to determine what happened in the past, why it happened, and how it has affected the present and may affect the future. After collecting data by reading vast amounts of material, historians analyze the information and then present it in the form of textbooks, lectures, studies, reports, and articles.

Most historians, more than 70 percent of them, are college teachers who research and write as well as carry out their teaching duties. The remaining historians work at jobs where their historical skills and knowledge are required. This may mean writing histories for companies and governmental units. It can mean researching historical records for businesses, law firms, television or movie companies, and public agencies. It can also mean analyzing past trends for banks, insurance companies, investment services, manufacturers, utilities, and public relations firms. No matter where a historian works, the job is ideal for bookworms because it always allows them to read while doing their jobs.

Education and Job Opportunities

Because most historians work as college teachers, a doctorate in history is almost essential to obtain employment. Teaching jobs open up when faculty members retire or enrollment in history courses increases.

Opportunities to obtain a position as a historian are quite limited. Overall, fewer than one thousand job openings for historians occur each year. There is keen competition for these openings, whether they are at colleges, museums, archives, historical societies, businesses, or with the government. Only a few historians are self-employed as writers, consultants, or researchers.

A Historian in Women's Studies

Until recently, the role of women has been overlooked in history. There was a dearth of material written on this subject. Sara Evans, a University of Minnesota professor, is a historian who recognized that the history of women was undervalued. Hired by the university to teach women's history, Sara combined this job with the writing of scholarly works on women. Her approach is not to romanticize the role of women by telling of heroines but to prove that women whose names aren't household words have helped to shape the United States.

Sara's research has taken her to libraries, museums, and archives to answer questions about the past. An important part of her research has been figuring out what type of material to study. For example, to find out about the diet and workload of slaves, her students have studied plantation records.

Both Sara's teaching duties and research in women's studies have entailed considerable reading. Obviously, historians are readers; however, the time Sara spends reading varies enormously. When she is on leave, she reads as much as forty hours a week. The pluses to her work are that she feels she is doing something new all the time and that her work is making a difference in the way people see the past.

Researchers for Publishers

When you read an article in an encyclopedia, the *New Yorker*, *National Geographic*, *Newsweek*, or *Time*, you expect the facts to be accurate. There is a small brigade of workers at these organizations who research to make sure that the facts you read are accurate. They are seekers of the truth, whether their job titles are fact checkers, junior researchers, or senior researchers. These researchers spend their days reading and phoning as they go over articles word by word to make them reliable.

The backgrounds of these researchers vary. However, a knowledge of research techniques and an insatiable desire to find the true facts are essential. It is also necessary to be able to write clearly because these researchers must explain proposed changes.

Researching for an Encyclopedia Publisher

As a child, Cheryl Graham would read Nancy Drew books and dream of being a detective. Today, as chief researcher of special projects for World Book, she fulfills that dream as she acts as a sleuth digging up hard-to-find facts for the encyclopedia and other publications. Being a fact detective involves using the computer to research current information. Online, Cheryl visits many different websites, including those of newspapers, news wires, governmental bodies, and universities. When looking up historical information, she is more apt to use printed sources and may visit special libraries. Half of Cheryl's time is spent researching major encyclopedia articles on topics such as individual countries, drug abuse, and evolution. The rest of her time is spent checking the facts of articles submitted by contributors for special World Book publications. It may take her a day to check the facts on a biographical sketch of Frank Gehry, the famous architect who designed the art museum in Bilbao, Spain. However, a lengthy article on environmental pollution could require as long as a month to check the facts thoroughly because it involves talking with experts and finding many different sources.

All of Cheryl's jobs have involved considerable reading. At her first job with the Library of Congress, she set up a library for congressional staffers doing research on environmental policy. This meant sitting down and reading articles like crazy so she could abstract and index them. She then worked at two other libraries as a reference librarian before coming to World Book.

This bookworm never tires of looking up interesting facts and reading about them. Cheryl's job as a researcher has become more interesting as the breadth of her knowledge increases. Her on-the-job reading has lead her to latch onto subjects and pursue them further in her free time. As a result, she has become an expert in several topics, including historical textiles.

··

Information Brokers

When businesses, organizations, and even individuals need specific information to solve problems or answer questions, they call on information brokers. Being an information broker is essentially being a researcher. It is also being a reader because brokers use libraries and online databases to find specific information for their clients. Some brokers specialize in a particular area, such as the environment, biotech, or patents. Careers in information brokering have really just emerged in the past thirty years. Choose a career in this area, and you will probably work alone; there are few information-brokering companies. And each job will bring a new challenge to find information, so you will never be bored. To be a successful information broker, you need solid research skills, computer expertise, and the ability to market yourself. About half of all information brokers are librarians. The rest are experienced in specific subject areas.

A Super Internet Searcher

Fellow information brokers describe Mary Ellen Bates as a super Internet searcher because of her expertise in finding information for businesspeople online. She is the proprietor and sole employee of her own research and consulting business, started in Washington, D.C., in 1991. Most of Mary Ellen's time on the job is spent sitting in front of the computer, as she uses online databases as well as such resources as trade association and government agency sites on the Internet.

Mary Ellen does most of her research reading online. Besides reading, Mary Ellen must analyze, synthesize, and package what she has read for her clients. In addition, she has the responsibility of doing all the myriad tasks required to operate a successful business, which takes approximately three hours a day. Part of this time is devoted to marketing activities, participating in E-mail discussion groups, and volunteering for professional associations. Mary Ellen also spends time reading print materials such as the *Wall Street Journal*, *Wired*, *Information Advisor*, and *Searcher* magazines, as well as online magazines and a number of professional listservs to keep current professionally.

In the future, Mary Ellen feels the need for information brokers will accelerate as more and more people discover how difficult it is to access accurate information quickly. She believes prospective information brokers will find courses in business helpful, as they will be running a business. Plus, Mary Ellen advises joining the Association of Independent Information Professionals to gain access to solid advice from those already in this profession. You can write to:

Association of Independent Information Professionals
7044 South Thirteenth Street
Oak Creek, WI 53154
www.aiip.org

For Further Reading

So much of research involves reading. Here is a job that truly allows bookworms to combine avocation with vocation. The following books provide additional information on careers in research.

Basch, Reva, and Mary Ellen Bates. *Researching Online for Dummies*. Foster City, CA: IDG Books Worldwide, 2000.

Bates, Mary Ellen. *Super Searchers Cover the World*. Medford, NJ: Information Today, 2001.

McGann, James G., and R. Kent Weaver, eds. *Think Tanks & Civil Societies: Catalysts for Ideas and Action.* Piscataway, NJ: Transaction Books, 2000.

Paige, Loraine. *Super Searcher, Author, Scribe.* Medford, NJ: Information Today, 2002.

Sacks, Risa. *Super Searchers Go to the Source: The Interviewing and Hands-On Information Strategies of Top Primary Researchers—Online, on the Phone, and in Person.* Chicago: Independent Publishers Group, 2001.

CHAPTER EIGHT

Careers with the Government

Reading for the Public Interest

F ew people are aware of all the vital services that federal, state, and local governments provide to them. The federal government defends us from foreign aggression, represents our interests abroad, enforces laws, and administers many different programs and agencies. Did you realize that it is the federal government that makes sure that we have reliable weather forecasts and can purchase uncontaminated food? Closer to home, state and local governments are providing us with such services as transportation, public safety, health care, education, and courts.

Federal, state, and local governments employ people in occupations that are found in nearly every industry in the country as well as in many jobs that are only found in the public sector. Many of the close to twenty million civilian government workers have jobs that fit the bill for those who are bookworms. The job opportunities for bookworms are enormous, as federal, state, and local governments hire thousands of new employees each month.

Jobs in the public sector offer certain advantages. First of all, there is usually more long-term job security than in the private sector. Although most public service jobs pay salaries slightly lower than those earned in the private sector, the benefits may be more generous in the public sector, especially vacation, sick leave, and retirement benefits. In addition, employees can often count on cost-of-living adjustments and merit raises. Plus, many jobs offer the chance to work flexible hours. There is also the inviting opportunity to get considerable responsibility early in your career.

Working for the Federal Government

Most jobs with the federal government are found in the executive branch, which has almost three million civilian employees. They work in more than nine hundred different occupations for more than 150 agencies and departments. Executive branch employees don't just work in Washington, D.C. In fact, close to 90 percent work in other geographical areas, including those who work abroad. What's more, you can often keep the same job and move from state to state or even city to city.

Although people tend to think that the number of people working for the federal government is growing rapidly, this is certainly not true. The period of rapid growth was the 1960s and 1970s. Since then, federal employment has not grown as rapidly as nonfederal employment. Still, many jobs are available, especially as replacements. Frequently, as many as twenty-five thousand people are hired by the federal government in a month.

How to Find Out About Jobs

Perhaps one of the hardest things to do is to find out where the jobs in government are that would appeal to you as a bookworm. In general, the occupational groups where you will find these jobs are GS-0100 (social science, psychology, and welfare), GS-0300 (general administrative, clerical, and office services), GS-1000 (information and arts), GS-1400 (library and archives), and GS-1800 (investigation group). You can learn more about these jobs by reading books or online guides with job descriptions.

After you have an idea of what kind of job you are looking for, you have the difficult task of finding out where vacancies for those jobs exist. The federal government is quite decentralized, so you can't just go to one spot and find out about all the jobs that are available. A few job vacancies are advertised in newspapers. You can also find a limited number of listings in professional journals. A college placement office is another place to find out about certain positions. In addition, state employment offices have lists of vacancies. And some federal buildings have touch-screen computers with employment information. The most complete and up-to-date job information is found online. One site that you should visit is the United States Office of Personnel Management (OPM) website at www.opm.gov. For job information with a specific agency, it is always a good idea to visit its regional office because agencies must post all their vacancies. You can find the addresses and phone numbers of government agencies online or at a public library.

How to Get a Job

Whenever you find out about a job opening, you should get a copy of the vacancy announcement. It will give you all the details you need to apply successfully for the job. It provides the exact identifying number of the job, which you must have because the same job could be found in more than one agency. It lists the deadlines for submitting applications and helpful information on salary, job title, number of positions available, the location of the job, the job description, and the qualifications required. This announcement can be obtained from the agency that has the vacancy as well as from the agency's website.

To apply for most jobs in the federal government, you now have two options. You can complete the OF 612 application form or write your own federally structured resume that must include forty-two required items. Rather than just completing an application or resume once, a master should be created that can be revised to suit each job you apply for. This is because applications are evaluated for each job on the basis of the job's duties and your qualifications. Most agencies also expect you to answer specific questions on a blank sheet of paper about your knowledge, skills, abilities, and other characteristics (KSAO). The KSAO may play the most important role in determining whether you are considered eligible for a job. Besides formally submitting an application for a job, it is also helpful to contact individuals who hire at agencies that interest you for advice, information, and possible interviews. Another way to get your foot in the door for a job in any branch of the federal government is by obtaining an internship. Not only will you learn firsthand what different government jobs are like, you will also become acquainted with the individuals who are doing the hiring for many positions.

Government Jobs That Pay You to Read

Jobs that involve doing studies and research—and there are many in these categories within the federal government—are the ones that are literally going to pay you to read. One such job is as a social science analyst. There are thousands of jobs in this category located in different government units throughout the country. Because this position is very desirable, the competition for entry-level positions is keen. Many successful job seekers have master's degrees when only a bachelor's degree is required.

Another area in which bookworms may find jobs is within the intelligence community. This includes the Central Intelligence Agency, the Federal Bureau of Investigation, the Drug Enforcement Agency, and other related agencies. The National Archives, presidential libraries, the Smithsonian Institution, and the National Trust for Historic Preservation are additional places where bookworms should look for jobs.

Jobs in the Legislative and Judicial Branches

Although the lion's share of jobs in the federal government is found in agencies of the executive branch, jobs in the legislative and judicial branches are also available. You can find out about these jobs in some of the same ways that you find out about jobs in the executive branch. However, you have to contact each legislative agency to find out about specific job vacancies and hiring procedures. Many of the agencies have job hot lines. On the legislative side, bookworms are most likely to find appealing jobs at the General Accounting Office, the Library of Congress, the Government Printing Office, and the Congressional Budget Office.

Jobs at the Library of Congress

An excellent place for bookworms to find jobs is in the Congressional Research Service of the Library of Congress. Hundreds of social science analysts are employed here to give members of Congress and congressional committees information and to make impartial analyses of pending policy issues. Analysts might be assigned to find out what the alternatives are to the current structure of congressional committees or the ways in which affordable housing can best be provided. The analysts do research, compile materials, and gather the pros and cons on an issue. A senior researcher may put together his or her own data. Entire days can be spent doing nothing but on-the-job reading.

Jobs on Capitol Hill

Senators and representatives have offices both in Washington, D.C., and in their home districts. The Washington staffs are larger and are better job bets for bookworms because they have staff members who do some research. If you want a job with a senator or representative, it doesn't hurt to go to the congressperson's office. There is an unbelievable amount of competition for staff vacancies, and it can be helpful to have made contact with those who are doing the hiring.

Bookworms can also find jobs on legislative committees and subcommittees that require people who are experts in certain policy areas. Both the House and Senate have referral services where you can fill out applications or submit them online, and they will be circulated to congressional offices, committees, and subcommittees. For information about the referral services, contact:

U.S. House of Representatives
Office of Human Resources
Ford House Office Building, Room 175
Washington, DC 20515
www.house.gov/cao-hr

Senate Placement Office
Hart Senate Office Building, Room 175
Washington, DC 20510
www.yourcongress.com

Working for State Governments

There are actually more jobs at the state level than at the federal level. Many of these jobs are in higher education and libraries, which are favorite places for bookworms to work. Jobs at the state level in the executive, legislative, and judicial branches are similar to those in the federal government except that they obviously do not deal with international relations, nor do they usually pay as well.

You will find announcements of jobs in state government in many of the same ways that you find announcements of federal jobs. In addition, you will find job announcements in such places as bulletin boards in government buildings, public libraries, and community organizations. After you have found the announcement of a job that appeals to you, follow the instructions on the announcement to submit your application. It is also a good idea to contact people at agencies who are doing the hiring for job information.

Some State Jobs for Bookworms

Look for jobs for social science analysts because these jobs require considerable reading on the state level just as they do on the federal level. In most states, you will find some of these jobs in legislative auditors' offices. As an analyst, you would determine how well state programs, such as welfare or highway maintenance, are working. Then you would write reports to give this information to the legislature. Job requirements for this position usually are a master's degree in an area such as public affairs, economics, political science, or one of the social sciences plus some research experience. You can sometimes get a temporary position on a project that will lead to full-time employment.

Another state job that requires reading is legislative analyst for a house or senate research department. These analysts draft bills and amendments, summarize bills, and do research studies. They apply academic research to public policy. Holders of these jobs have master's degrees or are lawyers. Knowing how to use a computer is essential.

Working for Local Governments

The largest number of people are employed in local governments—the cities, towns, counties, townships, and school districts. It is at this level that you can work closest to the people. The greatest number of employees in this group are teachers. Finding and getting a job at this level is often a very informal process, especially in very small governmental units. Larger units have personnel departments that have vacancy announcements.

A Reader's Career in the Public Sector

Being a curious person who is constantly reading has allowed Carson Ford to hold several excellent jobs in the public sector even though she is not a college graduate. Her career also demonstrates the wide variety of jobs bookworms can find in this arena.

After ten years in advertising, Carson opted to work in the public sector because she wanted a more meaningful job that offered opportunities for personal growth. Her background helped her obtain a job with the state as director of the Soldiers and Sailors Monument Restoration Project in Indianapolis, Indiana. This project required raising $12 million. The lieutenant governor and his office were responsible for raising the corporate dollars, and Carson had the task of raising the grassroots dollars. She decided to get the Indiana schoolchildren involved because all Indiana students throughout the state study Indiana history in the fourth grade. Ball State University faculty helped her develop a curriculum on the history of the monument and the Civil War. The director's job was perfect for a bookworm, as Carson was required to get very involved in reading about the Civil War and the history of the monument in order to be able to raise the money for the restoration. In two years, the fund-raising goal was accomplished.

With her solid experience at the state level, Carson was able to move easily to the local level, becoming the executive director of the Greater Indianapolis Progress Committee, a bipartisan advisory board to the mayor of Indianapolis. Again, Carson was constantly reading on the job to learn more about the issues that would lead to the rebirth of downtown Indianapolis. After six years in this job, Carson became the executive director of the Heartland Film Festival. This was a fun job because her mission was to promote life-affirming films for the Indianapolis festival, which was held once a year for a week in October. It was also a challenging job because she was the first director and had the responsibility of organizing the festival.

After two years with the festival organization, Carson returned to working for the state as director of resource development at the Pleasant Run Children's Home. In this job, she did all the home's marketing and fund-raising. There was also a lot of reading because Carson had to learn about the field of abused and neglected children. During her years in this position, Carson feels that some of her best reading was the essays and poems written by the children at the treatment facility. Because reading resources were limited for the children, this bookworm started a library and made sure that every child received a new book for the holidays. She had the children in the program serve as the librarians—cataloging and checking the books in and out.

Continuing in the state government arena, Carson's present job as executive director of the Indiana Literacy Foundation is the perfect job for a reader because it requires her to spend much of her day reading as she looks for money. Appropriately, this is also a job in which she promotes reading. Carson says that she could not handle this part of the job unless she herself was a reader. Reading is such a way of life for her that off the job she is currently reading nonfiction, fiction, and history books.

Working as an Elected Official

Some elected officials find themselves absolutely drowning in materials to be read. Most legislators, at all government levels, can never get all job-related reading done. The president, governors, and mayors of large cities all have so much reading to do that they frequently ask assistants to limit reports to one-page summaries. Judges also must necessarily spend much of their time reading.

For Further Reading

Because the federal government has so many jobs and hiring practices vary so much, bookworms who want to find jobs that let them read are going to have to do a lot of reading to find those jobs. It is absolutely essential to have an understanding of how the government works. In addition, you need to read books like the following ones that explain about the government and governmental jobs.

Damp, Dennis. *Book of U.S. Government Jobs: Where They Are, What's Available and How to Get One.* McKees Rock, PA: Bookhaven Press, 2002.

Goldenkoff, Robert, and Dana Morgan, eds. *Federal Jobs: The Ultimate Guide.* New York: Macmillan General Reference, 2002.

Guide to America's Federal Jobs. Indianapolis: JIST Publishing, 2001.

Rowh, Mark; Larry E. Naake; and Neale J. Baxter. *Opportunities in Government Careers.* Chicago: VGM Career Books, 2001.

Troutman, Kathryn Kraemer. *Federal Resume Guidebook.* Indianapolis: JIST Publishing, 1999.

CHAPTER NINE

Careers in the Private Sector

Reading for the Profit Makers

As a bookworm, you are most likely to work in the private sector because this is where nine out of ten jobs are. It is difficult to predict exactly what you will do, as consumer demand and new technology strongly influence where the greatest number of jobs are. One thing is certain: education will pay dividends in finding a job in the private sector in the future. The fastest growing job areas are those that require employees to have associate's or bachelor's degrees. You have already read about careers in publishing, education, research, and glamour industries. Now, you will find out about the professional and business jobs that should be filled by people who love to read.

With the constant explosion of new technology and knowledge in almost every field, few employees can afford not to read to keep up with what is happening in their areas of employment. The secret is to find the jobs that require more than routine reading. Quite often these jobs are to be found in areas where research is done.

If a bookworm has a specific field of interest, it may be possible to turn this interest into a job asset. The reader who has developed an in-depth knowledge of an industry, a country, or a product is a more attractive candidate for a job than someone who will have to learn vital background information on the job.

Reading Jobs in Traditional Professions

Occupations that require advanced education and training and also involve intellectual skills—such as medicine, law, engineering, theology, and teaching—are regarded as professions. If you have an intense interest in one of these professions, it is possible to find a job within it that lets you read. Because many professions allow one to be self-employed, you can also tailor your job to fit your love of reading.

Doctors Read

Doctors who teach and those who work at research institutions spend much of their time reading—not only to increase understanding but also in order to write papers. Even a doctor who primarily treats patients finds it essential to do at least four or five hours a week of solid professional reading beyond the routine reading of charts.

Lawyers Read

The younger lawyers are, the more they read because they need to do more research. It is not unusual for a junior attorney in a law firm to spend three or four hours a day reading briefs and cases. In addition, law clerks for judges, especially appellate judges, do a lot of reading. As lawyers become more senior, their reading time decreases. Still, most read for one or two hours a day, and it is not unusual for them to read three or more. Nowadays, more and more of this reading is done on computers rather than in law books because information can be accessed faster in this way.

Lawyers do not just practice law. One job that requires a legal background as well as very intense reading is putting head notes on cases for publishers of law books. Another job is as a teacher in a law school.

Engineers Read

A career as an engineer could be in any one of twenty-five major specialties, which are further divided into numerous subdivisions. Engineers must read to keep abreast of the latest scientific discoveries in their fields because engineers are often the link between scientific discoveries and their applications. They must learn about such things as the development of new and improved materials in order to design and build machinery, roads, bridges, power plants, cars, factories, and products. While their reading is concentrated on technical journals, engineers must also read to learn about governmental regulations affecting their work, especially in the area of environmental concerns.

Members of the Clergy Read

Reading for members of the clergy can be for contemplation, gathering information for sermons, learning more about one's faith, and increasing knowledge in an area like counseling.

Stockbrokers and Financial Analysts Read

When people buy stocks and bonds (securities), they usually deal with stockbrokers. Because things are always changing so fast in these markets, brokers have to snatch every moment they can to keep up with what is happening. Unfortunately, not too much of this can take place during the day when the market is open and they are busy dealing with clients. Also, because they receive reams of material to digest, stockbrokers must skim much of what they read.

If you are fascinated by what is happening in the securities market, there are analyst jobs in the investment area that are made just for bookworms. On the sell side, the jobs are with brokerage firms and investment banks that sell securities to investors; on the buy side, the jobs are with bank trust departments, insurance companies, and fund management firms.

On the sell side, analysts focus on areas such as faster transaction processing, trade execution, and global fulfillment for their firms' clients. On the buy side, analysts spend their time figuring out what should be bought and sold for their firms' portfolios. On either side, knowledge increases the probability that a decision will be a correct one.

Analysts read constantly to stay up-to-date with what is happening because things change every day. Stocks and bonds that appear to be an excellent investment at the start of a week may be a poor choice by the end of the week.

Most analysts are assigned a specific industry. Within that area, they will read all the information that they can get their hands on about the industry, firms in the industry, related government regulations, and world events that may affect the industry. Weather, revolutions, and governmental policy changes are just a few of the events that can change the value of securities. Besides reading, much time is spent talking to people to find out what is happening. After gathering information, analysts write reports to share that information.

If you decide to work as an analyst in the securities industry, you are likely to be working in New York City, which is the financial headquarters for more firms than any other place. It is important for you to know that employment in these firms is very cyclical. When times are good, employment is up. After contractions in the market, the number of employees is quickly reduced.

There is a very high level of competition for positions as analysts in the securities industry. It is possible for recent college graduates to enter this field and learn on the job. However, senior analysts usually have master's degrees in business. More and more also have attained the professional designation of Chartered Financial Analyst (CFA), which is obtained after passing a series of three tests and showing experience in the field.

Bank Economists Read

Like stockbrokers and financial analysts, the management team at a bank needs to know what is happening around the world in the economy. At banks that have $10 billion or more in deposits, there are staff economists. The chief economist is likely to have a doctorate in economics. Assistants probably also have advanced degrees. However, there are entry-level jobs for college graduates with majors in economics. At all levels, economists read so they can write reports on the economy for the bank and its clients.

....

Jobs in Information Services

Among the fastest-growing businesses in the economy are the information services companies that generate, process, and distribute data. With the world just about drowning in information, businesses, schools, professional people, the government, and even students researching papers need help to quickly find information. And this demand for information continues to accelerate each year, especially as more and more information is placed on the Internet.

Information services professionals get paid to read about the arts, environment, photography, and many other topics. Many work as indexers and abstractors for information services companies, where they read journals, magazines, and newspapers; organize bibliographic information; and write abstracts for articles. Writing an abstract involves reflecting the author's opinion. Many companies have a training period for this job during which employees learn editorial policy, what goes into abstracts, how to organize and select material, and how to avoid plagiarism. Of course, you have to love to read to enjoy this job. Other job requirements include a college degree, expertise in grammar, computer literacy, and an ability to record information accurately.

At some information services companies, you must work on-site. Others let you work at home and send your work in by modem. Although there are deadlines, you are often free to structure the hours you work. This flexibility makes the job appealing to many people, and the nature of the work itself is perfectly suited to bookworms.

A Political Analyst

Julie Sedky reads from 40 to 50 percent of the time on her job as a political analyst at a firm that does public policy research for institutional investors. She tries to anticipate and analyze changes in governmental policy that will affect her clients, who invest other people's money and don't want to be surprised by what happens in Washington, D.C. She regularly reads such material as the *Washington Post, Wall Street Journal, Bureau of National Affairs Daily Report for Executives, Congressional Quarterly,* and the *Economist,* as well as excerpts from the *Congressional Record,* materials put out by the Congressional Budget Office and congressional leaders, and a number of private newsletters that tell what's going on in Washington, D.C. Julie's expertise in finding information is such that she sometimes finds her own words in references.

Jobs for Consultants

Consultants act as problem solvers in both the public and private sectors. They are also hired to do work similar to that done in think tanks. Being a consultant means doing research and analysis for a client. It could involve determining how a scarcity of labor would affect a firm. It might be a question of determining what the major trends in an industry are. No matter what the task, the major tool for accomplishing it is always reading.

While consulting firms vary in size from one-person operations to large international corporations, it is at the larger firms that most entry-level positions are found. Recent college graduates can often find jobs as assistants on projects.

Jobs in Corporate America

The companies that make automobiles, soap, frozen dinners, and paper, as well as the companies that drill for oil or build airplanes, have jobs for bookworms. No matter what it produces, if the company is large enough, there will be jobs that require reading. When you look for a job in corporate America, be sure to investigate areas such as human resources, marketing, and consumer relations.

Human Resources Employees Read

All the hiring and firing of employees, the negotiating of labor agreements, and the determining of benefits and salaries are done in the human resources department at a large company. This is the department that deals with all the people who work at a company. Because the federal government as well as state governments have many laws that spell out exactly how employees are to be treated, employees in this department must do a lot of reading just to keep up with statutory requirements. Then they have to make sure that the people in operations know what these laws are and follow them.

Terri Nelson works for a Fortune 500 company as a placement specialist. This is not a job that you can just step into because so many companies want college graduates who have experience, and there are few training positions. Many placement specialists begin as clerical workers to get basic business experience. Terri, who has a college degree, worked as a secretary in human resources, a bookkeeper, and a customer service representative before becoming a placement specialist.

During a typical week, Terri may read as many as five hundred resumes of people seeking employment with her company. She is looking for people who meet the qualifications for positions that are available. She reviews the resumes of all the qualified candidates for a position and then writes down questions to ask each of these applicants. She also interviews applicants and conducts an orientation program for new employees.

Terri estimates that she reads 70 to 80 percent of the time on the job. Besides reading resumes, she keeps up with the literature in her field and reads government rulings.

Market Developers Read

In his career in market development for a television network, Michael Sanchez and his team members negotiate agreements with hundreds of cable and satellite providers and develop marketing initiatives to promote products and services for the network and its affiliates. It is extremely helpful that Michael has always loved to read because he probably spends five hours a day reading on the job. Although this is not reading the novels that he loves, his ability to read fast to absorb information about past and current business relationships has contributed to his own success as well as the continued success of his company.

Michael explains that it is imperative for him to read on the job because the television network business is always changing—new technologies, new partners, and new competitors. He points out that reading is especially critical when it comes to contracts. When he says "reading," it sometimes means reading the same contract over and over and over! The words don't change, but his interpretation just might. During a typical day on the job, he reads forty or fifty E-mails, two newspapers, and the trade publications in his career area (*Variety, MultiChannel News, CableFax*), along with some news and entertainment magazines and four or five contracts and/or reports.

Marketing Researchers Read

Some companies use information services to find out about marketing trends or how consumers like a product. Other companies have their own marketing research departments and may also use information services. Jobs in marketing research involve keeping in touch with what consumers want through test marketing and product testing. This includes collecting data through research and reading. The background needed for this job varies from company to company. Many market researchers have a bachelor's degree in business and an advanced degree in marketing, finance, or accounting.

Consumer Relations Workers Read

When consumers are unhappy, they write to companies to voice their complaints. Companies receive mail asking why a prize was not included in a cereal box as promised or complaining that a new car has needed numerous adjustments. Companies also receive mail asking for information about such things as products or company activities. Letters may ask why a product isn't biodegradable or why a company is doing business with a certain country.

To keep their customers' goodwill, employees in customer relations departments answer all of these letters. Some employees read and answer mail all day, while others alternate between handling mail and fielding telephone calls. Many letters can be answered with personalized form letters. Answering some letters requires research. Companies try to answer every letter as accurately as possible.

To get a job answering mail or the telephone, it is not always necessary to have a college degree. In addition, here is a job where experience is not required. Employees do have to demonstrate an ability to write.

....

For Further Reading

Because the private sector is where most of the jobs are, this is the area where bookworms should do the most reading. Investigate what careers in different professions offer as well as what jobs with financial institutions and information services are like. Finally, read to find out what jobs are available in corporate America. Reading the following books is just a starting point for learning about jobs in the private sector.

Careers in Focus: Business. Chicago: J. G. Ferguson Publishing Company, 2000.

Clark, Val. *Getting & Keeping the Job: Success in Business & Technical Careers.* New York: Allyn & Bacon, 2002.

Farr, Michael. *America's Top 300 Jobs.* Indianapolis: JIST Publishing, 2002.

Henry, Maxye, and Lou Henry. *101 Tips for Running a Successful Home Business.* Chicago: VGM Career Books, 2000.

Stair, Lila B. *Careers in Business.* Chicago: VGM Career Books, 1998.

VGM Careers Encyclopedia. Chicago: VGM Career Books, 2002.

CHAPTER TEN

More Career Opportunities for Bookworms

Discovering Additional Options

Bookworms will most certainly find true happiness in their careers if they can find jobs that will let them read from nine to five. As you have discovered in this book, there are many careers in which you will actually be paid to read. Doing some additional reading will lead you to even more careers. Browse through an occupational handbook or jobs guide while thinking of your fondness for reading as well as your interests and skills to discover more possibilities. Expand your options further by reading want ads in newspapers and professional journals and visiting online job sites. Remember, it may take some creativity to find a job that matches your interests and abilities. Here are a few more careers that other bookworms have found to be quite satisfying.

Translator

A good translator needs to be able to change the written word from one language to another. In order to do this, a translator really needs to be a bookworm in two languages. Translators are especially in demand in businesses, government agencies, and research organizations. Many also freelance or work for translation services. This is a job that offers both full-time and part-time employment. Bookworms in this field need to be prepared to read all kinds of scientific, technical, commercial, and legal material.

....

Braille Transcriber

You will not get rich being a braille transcriber, but you will be providing a very important service to blind people who read braille. Braille transcribers turn the printed word on all kinds of subjects into braille. This can be done by using six of the regular keys and the function keys on a computer or less commonly by using a device called a braillewriter. Braille transcribing also can be done by just typing exact copy and using special computer programs. However, a trained braillist must know how to format the copy correctly in braille.

To become truly proficient in transcribing braille can take several years. Most transcribers take a class so they can become certified by the Library of Congress. To gain certification, you have to submit an almost perfect forty-page document in braille. You can find jobs as a braille transcriber with braille book publishers and state departments of education. Most of this work is done on a freelance basis, so you can work at home. School districts also have jobs for transcribers that involve visiting schools and preparing teacher handouts and quizzes for those students who need the work in braille. Furthermore, there are many opportunities to transcribe braille as a volunteer.

....

Books-on-Tape Reader

If you have an excellent reading voice, you may be able to find a job that pays you for reading aloud. As you have probably noticed, more and more books are now available on audiocassettes. People who make these recordings can earn hundreds of dollars a day. The problem is that obtaining one of these jobs is extremely difficult. Many readers are professional actors and broadcasters.

Furthermore, recording studios are generally located only in metropolitan areas.

Recorder for the Blind and Dyslexic

Although you will not get paid to make recordings for the blind and dyslexic, it can be a very satisfying activity for bookworms of all ages. Several organizations can give you information about making these recordings. One organization is Recording for the Blind & Dyslexic, which will give you the phone number of one of its thirty-six studios that make these recordings so you can obtain an information packet for volunteer readers. Write to:

Recording for the Blind & Dyslexic
20 Roszel Road
Princeton, NJ 08540
www.rfbd.org

You will need to pass a vocal test to become a volunteer. Your first task will be to learn how to interpret all the marks so you will know how to read the text. Volunteers are then required to read at least two hours a week and will usually read textbooks. If you are reading textbooks in subject areas such as calculus and chemistry, you will need to be knowledgeable about the subject in order to explain the illustrations and symbols used in these books.

Genealogist

People want to know where their great-grandmothers were born and what their great-great-grandfathers did for a living. Genealogists help people learn about their ancestors. They research for clues in libraries, church records, courthouses, old letters, diaries, newspaper clippings, census records, and government archives. Much of the work can be done online. This job requires keeping careful records. It also requires people who like to work alone; most genealogists are self-employed. There are no formal educational requirements for becoming a genealogist. Although there are some courses in genealogy that can be helpful, most people acquire job knowledge through other genealogists and reading material on genealogy.

Abstractor

If you enjoy independent research and doing very exacting work, you might like to be an abstractor for an abstract or title insurance company. This work involves finding all the records on a piece of property so a clear title can be issued when it is sold. Abstractors search through dusty volumes in the basements of courthouses and also use computers to find this information. They never stop reading all day long. Although you don't have to have a college education to be an abstractor, some courses in law, real estate, and business can be helpful. It takes from four to six years of on-the-job training to learn how to do all kinds of abstracts. Most abstractors work in metropolitan areas, where there are usually job openings for this position.

Accountant

You may think of accountants as being just number people. Nevertheless, this is also a job that requires considerable reading. Tax accountants must be up-to-date on the thousands of pages of federal and state regulations. Internal auditors have to make sure that companies are following corporate policies and government regulations. Plus, most states require public accountants and certified public accountants to take continuing education courses.

Word Processor

Word processing can just be transcribing work and putting it into an attractive format. Or it can involve editing and revising letters, reports, and other printed materials. Although it is a job that involves considerable reading, it is essentially clerical in nature. One advantage of this job is the possibility of doing it from your home as a telecommuter.

Nutritionist

Nutritionists and dietitians plan food and nutrition programs in many settings, from hospitals to schools to doctors' offices. Because the information on nutrition is constantly growing, they must do a lot of reading to meet the nutritional needs of those they serve. Lisa Mahan is a nutrition coordinator for a large cardiology practice. Her patients rely on her to sort through all the information published on health so that she can tell them what is appropriate for them. Lisa believes that she is always reading on the job, whether it is patient charts, online materials, books, journals, newsletters, or health magazines.

Judge

Television has brought judges and their work into your home. Outside of the courtroom, judges must spend considerable time reading documents on pleadings and motions. They also have to research legal issues. The amount of reading judges do varies by jurisdiction. General trial judges do not do as much reading as federal and state appellate court judges, who study lower-court decisions to see if they should be upheld or overturned.

Wire Editor

If you are curious about what is happening in Australia, South Dakota, and every corner of the world, being an editor for a news agency that distributes news and photographs to newspapers, radio and television stations, and news magazines is a good choice. These editors sit in front of a computer screen and read news. They pull copy and edit it and also route copy to clients. It is a job that lets you read for almost eight hours a day and also puts the news of the world at your fingertips.

Author

Without authors, there would be no books, magazines, textbooks, newsletters, pamphlets, bulletins, or newspapers for bookworms to read. Authors aren't just writers; most are bookworms, too. Think of all the research that has to be done by authors. Imagine how much reading James Michener had to do in order to write *Hawaii* or *Centennial*. Consider how much reading was done to write this book. And don't forget the tremendous amount of reading that authors of textbooks do. Indeed, being an author is a superb career for bookworms and other literary types.

Still More Career Options

The more you think about the different kinds of material that people read, the longer your list of careers for bookworms will become. There are people who make crossword puzzles and people who make all kinds of tests, from achievement tests to intelligence tests. Then there are people who clip what others have written for clipping services.

The Future for Bookworms

The future is bright for bookworms and other literate types seeking jobs that allow them to be paid for reading. Tomorrow's best jobs will be in areas that require education, and as a group bookworms tend to be well educated. Bookworms will find even more jobs in the future in banking, education, law, research, and management consulting. And they will find a bonanza of reading jobs within the rapidly growing information services industry. As far as the public sector goes, most of the growth in government jobs will be at the state and local levels.

The years ahead should offer bookworms more and more opportunities to combine avocation and vocation because the world is deluged with an ever-increasing volume of written and online information, which will increase the need for reading on the job. Bookworms can also anticipate that reading on the job will continue to mean doing more and more reading on computer screens. The future presents opportunities to do more reading in just about every career.

About the Authors

....

M arjorie Eberts and Margaret Gisler have been writing together professionally for twenty-two years. They are prolific freelance authors with more than seventy books in print. This is their twenty-fourth VGM Career Books title. It is also the second career book for which Kevin Crider has provided valuable assistance.

Writing this book was a special pleasure for Eberts and Gisler because they are decidedly bookworms. Investigating the many careers that require reading on the job let them spend hours reading—their favorite avocation. It also gave them the opportunity to learn more about the fascinating careers so many bookworms have.

Besides writing books, the two authors write the King Features syndicated "Dear Teacher" column that appears in newspapers throughout the country. They also give advice on education issues online at the Family Education Website.

Eberts is a graduate of Stanford University, and Gisler is a graduate of Ball State and Butler Universities. Both received their specialist degrees in education from Butler University. The authors have more than twenty years of experience as educators between them.